Damn The ALLEGATORS

by Joseph E. Carter

**Edited By
W. Horace Carter
Pulitzer Prize Winning Journalist**

Copyright 1989 by
Joseph E. Carter

First Printing 1989

Published
by
Joseph E. Carter, Albemarle, N.C. 28001

Library of Congress Card Number 88-083675

ISBN Number 0-937866-17-2

Printed in the United States of America
by
Atlantic Publishing Company.
Tabor City, North Carolina 28463

Cover designed by Brad Horton.
Photographs on the cover and inside are by various treasury agents.

Edited
by
W. Horace Carter,
Hawthorne, Florida 32640.

FOREWARD

Early in the law enforcement career of Joe E. Carter, his friends tell of the time he singlehandedly raided a small cockfight in the boondocks and arrested all six men present, even though half of them scattered into the woods. Astonished people asked him how in the world he managed to apprehend six violators by himself.

"Surrounded 'em," he quipped.

For the next 20 years Joe intensified his "surrounding" tactics and the reverberations have gonged new dimensions and new imprints in the periphery of law enforcement anals in the Southeastern USA. For much of that 20-year span, I sweated, froze, raided, battled, boozed, snafu-ed, playboyed, and you-name-it with him, with my admiration for the man soaring by the day. We are both now retired on full disability resulting from on-the-job injuries.

Joe was the hardest-working Treasury Dept. Federal Agents (Bureau of Alcohol Tax and Firearms) I have ever known or ever heard of. Superiors sometimes chided him about being impatient with associates and subordinates, who, although average and normal people, possessed only a fraction of Joe's energy, initiative, imagination and a long list of other attributes.

"Let's get on with it," became his verbal trademark.

Whenever the most difficult cases involving the most formidable violators came up, it was always Joe Carter whom the Brass assigned, for Joe never let them down. Joe never let anybody down.

Our Desk Wheels issued a 'Procedural Manual' to guide ATF field personnel and Joe could always be depended on to abide by the contents — as long as it did not interfere with his making a good criminal case. Hell, he ignored it. Brilliant and unorthodoxy towered over Joe like a mile-high aura.

One never knew quite what to expect with Joe, except

results and achievement. One thing I do know, however, is that what you read in the following pages is TRUE, because I was there during most of it. Incredible though some of it may be, it is starkly real, genuine, he-manistic adventures of unforgettable days without equal. Because there will never be another Joseph E. Carter.

No doubt about it, he was ATF's best criminal investigator in the Southeast, probably in the nation. His reputation extends to the outer limits. None of the current ATF agents, young or old, can hope for a higher compliment than to be compared with Joe Carter — in any way.

Today there are scores of us — retirees, agents, supervisors, informers, former violators, judges, DA's, lawyers, officers and friends — who will crawl through Hell and all of Georgia if Joe Carter beckons.

Joe has an undiminished built-in drive to excell in everything he undertakes. This book is a superb example of that characteristic.

C. Richard Hearn
507 16th Avenue
Jasper, Alabama 35501

INTRODUCTION

This book is a factual and shocking account of a small, elite segment of your "treasury men in action" in the fifties and sixties involved in the destruction of moonshine whiskey. It is profane, violent, vulgar and raw but it is that because that's the way it was. As the author, I do not want to be so profane, but to write it otherwise would be taking away its reality. The violence of the criminals and the lawmen is sometimes rampant and it actually appears that the roles of the hunter and the hunted are interchangeable at times. If this book had been purged of the salty language and the violence, it would be unworthy of publication.

This point is more clearly explained by my recollection of a trial many years ago. An old attorney addressed the audience of a superior court that was convened to try his client for the crime of rape, a capital offense.

> *"Ladies and gentlemen," he began. "My client is on trial for his life. We are desperate. We will defend ourself without limit. We will use the language that we must. We will not substitute a 'nice' word for a bad one. In plain words, we will not call 'peckers' cucumbers, nor 'pussys' cauliflowers. If you cannont hack this, then you should leave now."*

Sadly, I have seen too many comrades retire in bitterness because of selfish reasons like not getting this promotion or that assignment. I am thankful that I never suffered such emotions. I am thankful that the ATF and all its agents tolerated my efforts. As far as I know, I left with no enemies, even the ones that I have referred to as "bastards"—a pet name that I have a habit of using with no malice and definitely no intention to cast doubts on anyone's parentage. All these were my brethren and although I know that some didn't do as well as others, they were all my companions and I was ready to risk my life for any of them if necessary, and often did.

It would be impossible now for an officer of the law to risk (with success) some of the tactics that you will read about in this book. Officers would be imprisoned if they dared to try many of these things.

In my retirement, many friends have said to me, "With your experience, why don't you run for sheriff?"

My answer is always, "If I ran for the city limits, the whole town would be behind me."

I have hung up my guns.

ABOUT THE AUTHOR

During my lifetime, our country has been involved in three major wars: World War II, Korean War, and the Vietnam War.

I was thirteen years old at the beginning of WWII and seventeen when it ended. From the date of December 7, 1941, the day of the cowardly attack on Pearl Harbor, I was "on fire" throughout the war to go fight for my country. When I became seventeen, I begged my father to sign for me to volunteer for the army. "Army hell!" he said. "Get your ass back to the cottonfield and get ready to fight the damned boll weevils—you're too young to fight the Japs." WWII ended five months later, although the selective service system continued drafting eighteen year olds on a very much reduced scale.

On my eighteenth birthday, I registered for the draft, but with the fear that I would never be called. However, I learned that I could "volunteer" to be called by the draft board. This I did and was "drafted" in January 1949 for a specified period of twenty-one months in the active army, with a commitment thereafter to serve six years in an active army reserve or National Guard unit or eight years inactive reserve pool which required no drills or training, but simply just another name on a roster.

Late summer 1949 found me on a troop ship enroute to Pearl Harbor as a member of the 72nd Heavy Tank Battalion, 2nd Infantry Division. We had been trained extensively to make amphibious beach-head landings (in joint Army-Navy training) at guess where?—Wakiki Beach near Honolulu and Wailua Beach, Kauai, Hawaii. Just like in the movies!

We made the landings but sadly, while enroute to Hawaii, we were informed that the Secretary of the Army, Kenneth Royal, had ordered all draftees released from active service to reserve service after one year active duty.

Back at Ft. Lewis, Washington, I was released (honorably) in January 1950 instead of October 1950, which would have been the time, except for the Secretary of the Army's decision to reduce the active time from twenty-one months to twelve months. On returning to civilian life and with a military reserve commitment, I chose this active reserve program. There was more than one reason for this. First, the active reserve concept was that of having weekend "drills" or training in uniform and being ready to be ordered as a unit into active service in case of emergency. Too, we were paid $4.00 for each drill—big bucks!

The popular chief of police in my hometown, Albemarle, North Carolina, L. D. Cain, a charter member of the North Carolina Highway Patrol (motorcycle brigade) was a major in the U. S. Army Reserve and commanded an active unit, which I joined. The chief took an instant liking to me and offered me a job as a policeman. I accepted. Thereafter, I served with him in the military and as one of his policemen. He was one of the best all-round human beings that I have ever known.

The Korean conflict began in June, 1950. Still having the "hero complex," I was confident that our highly trained and organized unit would be ordered into the conflict. I waited and waited but we were not called. This was to me very disappointing because my friends who were on the rolls and were not paid for being in a unit were eventually ordered to active duty. There was a big flap in the Congress about this. My disappointment was somewhat relieved by the action I was beginning to enjoy as a policeman.

Had I been in my old outfit, 2nd Infantry Division, instead of being released after twelve instead of twenty-one months, there is a great chance that I wouldn't be alive. The division was used as a rear guard to protect the retreat of thousands and thousands of troops from the Yalu River when the damned chinks hit us to stop McArthur's conquest of North Korea. My division and masses of my friends in the 2nd were slaughtered.

After the Korean War, I remained in the active Army Reserve and obtained a mail-order commission through two series of tests. Eventually, as a captain, Military Police Corps, U.S. Army Reserve, I was company commander of a crack MP Reserve unit in Raleigh, North Carolina from 1962 to 1968.

As a result of the frustrating failure to topple certain major racketeers, as a special investigator for the U.S. Treasury Department, on or about 1965, and the result of losing my first marriage because of a stronger commitment to my job, and finally because of the remaining desire to fight for my country, personal ego, or whatever, I jumped on the Vietnam experience. The Department of the Army offered certain thirteen-month tours for reserve officers up through the rank of Major (which I was at that time) for certain branches, including military police. My request for a leave of absence was tentatively approved.

I filed a request and was ordered to take a physical, which I immediately did. My "jinx" obstacle to be a war hero was still alive. The army doctors turned me down because of high blood pressure. Again, perhaps Providence intervened. At that particular time, as a senior military police officer, I would probably have been stationed in Saigon where the greatest danger of being killed would have been for a VC terrorist to roll a grenade into a bar. The bottom line: I was not allowed to go to Vietnam. Again, Providence? Shortly thereafter, the Tet Offensive—whereby the VC and North Vietnamese Army turned the tide of the war by a saturation invasion into the southern cities, especially Saigon, previously somewhat immune from the heat of the battles. Many, many policemen, American military police, etc. were killed.

By this time, however, at the age of forty, I was a veteran of almost twenty years of "combat" with some of the most interesting of criminals. This had helped my feeling of being cheated out of the glory of war to subside

United States Treasury Department

Certificate of Award

To JOE E. CARTER

In recognition and appreciation for noteworthy contribution to the effective and efficient operation of the Treasury Department

Wilbur J. ___
Regional Commissioner

SUPERIOR PERFORMANCE AWARD

July 1965

IX

CHAPTER 1
A BRAND NEW DEPUTY

Near the end of a four-hour tour of the county's eight-pint joints, Sheriff Clem Harris outlined to me, his brand new twenty-five year old deputy, his number-one law enforcement problem—bootleg whiskey and the crime it generated. He revealed a few dozen behind-the-scenes manipulators with a trifling investment were well on their way to millionaire status in this dry county, to the detriment of everyone else.

He nodded through the windshield toward a decrepit farmhouse nestled among some trees, wild shrubs and vines. A heavily-traveled driveway connected it to the highway.

"The bastard who operates that place is the meanest and the scummiest of them all," the sheriff growled. "Lots of the trouble this community has to deal with originates right there. Yeah, he's the hardest one to catch we got in the county, a slippery sonofagun. I wish to God that place would burn to the ground—tonight!"

It did.

Next morning, the sheriff caught my eye with a subtle nod and I joined him in his private office in the one hundred-year-old courthouse on the square.

"Joe, now listen. Hell fire! What I said about that joint burning, it was...a-hem...sort'uv a figure of speech, you know. I appreciate such fierce dedication to good law enforcement, but you can't go around committing arson. Just suppose the operator had been in there sleeping?"

"Sheriff, I know these people don't occupy these old fire-trap buildings at night after sales hours," I said. After all, he had blamed the weakness of the law on the existence of the joints; also the rumored reputation about his being on payola. It needed to burn.

Of course, as all good officers do, I denied any wrongdoing. How should I know who burned it? I had already learned the name of the whole game is: **"I DENIES THE ALLEGATIONS AND DAMNS THE ALLEGATORS."** I had heard that in court often

1

enough. For the next twenty years I practiced it religiously.

No investigation was made in the fire incident. No one even bothered to worry about it. The big shot bootlegger who owned it merely moved into another old house with no appreciable interruption in his business. He didn't miss a sale.

Sheriff Harris almost waddled when he walked. Along with being short, he was fat, bald, sixtyish, and he squinted behind his rimless glasses. He had been elected sheriff after retiring from the hardware business following World War II. Relatively wealthy for the times, he played it straight as a stick in business dealings and also as chief executive law enforcement officer of the county. He had more moral and physical courage than any officer I have ever known. He didn't drink or gamble, was honest and a devout church goer and worker.

He had only one noticeable fault. He would screw a pile of rocks if he didn't think it had a snake in it.

He hired me as his second deputy, being authorized only two, after I had resigned from the city police force with three years service because pressure was applied against me by the city councilmen. The problem: I had somehow been given a job as policeman by mistake. I was a Republican, and it was just not permissible to give such a political plum ($180 a month) to a Republican. My impressive record of arrests of felons, completion of home study courses in criminology and character were completely ignored.

The sheriff leaned to look around me toward the court-house corridor. I turned and saw the brown-haired broad who worked in Social Services strut by. Sheriff Harris mumbled his usual lustful wishes.

"Sheriff, some day when that woman passes you are going to forget that your wife is with you and say what you just did," I admonished him.

"Son, I'm telling you the truth," he replied. "I love my wife very much, but if I could get a piece of that and there was absolutely no other way than to let my wife be there, I would go ahead and do it and let her watch."

Two-Hat McLeod bumbled in with a handful of papers from the jail office. A freckled six-footer, he had flashy eyes that never quite finished looking around in all the corners as if he suspected someone to pounce upon him. Most people connected with law enforcement called him "Two-Hat" because along with being chief deputy, he held down the onerous job of jailer, a gruesome

2

twenty-four-hour-a-day headache. Other people called him "Mack." His health had not been good since he and the sheriff were shot all to hell a couple of years earlier by a drunken bootlegger whom they went to arrest for beating his wife. After I came to work, Two-Hat tended to spend more time at the jail where he had living quarters.

That was okay with us, because Two-Hat didn't want to go along with some of our accepted practices.

One habit we had was carrying with us a stack of blank search warrants for on-the-spot completion and execution in emergencies. Some of the people being searched never could understand how we were so fast in obtaining the search warrant. Others never questioned it because they couldn't read anyway. In this case, you learned who the illiterate ones were in short order and then you could use any kind of paper. Some of the documents I remember that worked quite well were an insurance policy, an automobile title and, in one case, a repair invoice for the prowl car from the Chevrolet dealer.

It was usual reaction for such a victim to exhibit his awareness of his constitutional rights and say, "You can't search me unless you got papers."

When presented with the repair invoice, he took it, scanned it extremely closely, looking back and forth like he was watching a tennis match, and pretended to read it. Then he handed it back with a grin, "You sure have got the papers. Go ahead!"

Sometimes Two-Hat had to hire extra help at the jail, depending on the jail population and on his health. He had extra help the night we had the big fight in the jail, and it was lucky for Two-Hat, who wound up in the hospital with a bad case of shot nerves.

My partner Fred and I arrested a drunk. Five blocks from the jail, we heard the most ungodly noise imaginable, like a stampede of rebellious savages. A freshly recruited turnkey or jailer, whom I had never seen before, admitted us into the jail reception room. This giant must have stood six-eight and weighed 260. Although I was a midget at five-eleven and 190, I acted cocky around him. Besides, I had lifted weights for several years, earning quite a reputation at a local industry where I would show off by lifting a thirty-three-foot railroad iron with two men sitting on it, a total of 1,290 pounds. It was a simple hip and leg lift, only about two tons short of a world record. But local people didn't know that.

3

The big jailer asked us to help separate the two guys causing all the trouble. They were both three-time losers, prisoners just convicted in Greensboro on narcotics violations and deposited in our jail pending transfer to a federal prison. They were brothers. In those days you didn't hear much about drugs. But these guys were both addicts as well as pushers. They had been on heroin. It had worn off and they were suffering living hell.

They were together in the bull pen, adjacent to about a dozen small cells with doors into each from within the bull pen. This whole compound was within a large room, barred off with steel walls.

These two men had torn every sheet, mattress, pillow, bunk and all the plumbing fixtures into little pieces. They were breathing fire and foaming at the mouth. They screamed at the top of their lungs, cried and cussed everything and everybody. They shook the bars and begged us to come into the compound where they promised to tear us to bits. They reminded me very much of vicious dogs in advanced stages of rabies. They cursed my mother, my wife, and swore before God they would kill us then or later.

In twenty-four years as a law enforcement officer, I never owned a blackjack. There were only two occasions that I used any weapon to fight a man except with my bare hands. One was a huge black man whom I slugged with a pair of aluminum knucks. The other was a runty little sailor who came closer to defeating me than anyone I can remember. In his case, I rammed him with a straight right holding a roll of nickels. The jackass who told me how much force the nickels added to your punch failed to tell me how many of my own knuckles it would break.

I should have noticed how frightened the jailer was. But I was too shocked by the brutal violence exhibited by these crazy prisoners to notice it.

I walked to the large steel-barred door, took off my Sam Browne belt, revolver and blue coat, and laid them on the floor.

One of the wild vandals shouted in a shrill voice, "Good...good...good, you blue-bellied sonofabitch, you gonna be goddamn hero ain't you? Just open the fuggin' door and come on in. We'll kill you just as sure as there's a God in..."

I felt confident, even cocky, with all the muscle and bone of the jailer backing me up. And, too, I was getting tired of these bastards spouting out obscenities and taunts. I couldn't stop

4

myself now. I had to prove something to them.

The big turnkey opened the door and I walked in. Both men lunged headlong at me as I heard the loudest clanging of a jail door I have ever heard before or since. The door had an automatic spring lock. Fred had no chance of helping me, since he didn't know which of the forty keys on the ring to use. The turn-key just slumped to the floor and began crying hysterically.

The memory of that ensuing brawl made the so-called fight of the century between Tony Zale and Rocky Graziano seem like a scout-a-rama.

The first man, in his lunge, got it good with my devastating left hook and went down. Now, I thought, if I can only throw him into one of the little cells and lock him up, I'll only have one to go. I reached down, picked him up by the shirt-tail and the testicles. I never made it. As I cleared the floor with the body, the second prisoner hit me between the eyes with everything he had. The rest of the melee was savage.

They bit, hit, stomped, kicked, slugged, and tore at me for what seemed like an hour, but which must have been only a few minutes. It was a relatively even fight until the larger one finally succeeded in kicking me in the balls. This was very painful and it affected me emotionally. I really lost my temper. The fight lasted only two more blows. One for each of them and they were asleep, with bells ringing.

One stayed out only for a moment and hunched, lifted his head and began his violent cursing all over again. This caused me to deliver the only kick of my career to the ribs of a man who was down. But I wasn't sorry.

I locked him in a cell and examined the other. Before I could determine anything about his condition Fred bustled in and the turnkey sobbed, "Oh, Lord, you've killed him! Now we'll all go to jail! He's dead! He's dead!"

I told him to shut the hell up and go get a bucket of water. The poor slob was so addled he clambered down three flights of stairs without a thought of the elevator.

Fred and I left the guy lying on the floor and called the county doctor. He looked like he was dead. We reported the fight to the desk sergeant. He panicked. He was an old-time cop nervous and shaky at this point who had sucked the teats of the city taxpayers for thirty years. Once he shot and killed a seventeen year old kid who tried to stick up the local bank with a toy pistol. Sarge told me I was in real trouble. "Those men

5

were federal prisoners and you may have killed one of them. I would never have gone in that cell."

Fred said, "I know damn well you wouldn't, Sarge, you haven't got the guts."

I was still excited from the fight, hurting from the kick in the balls and the knots on my head, disgusted with the jailer and now pissed-off at the Sarge. "I don't give a damn. The sonofabitch deserved what he got," I snarled.

Soon I began to cool off, which brought the realization that I might really have screwed up. I was afraid to go back to see what had happened. But I realized that I had to go and see for myself. Shifts were changing and no one else seemed concerned.

I went back to the jail. The turnkey was nowhere to be found. I picked up the ring of keys and went to the third floor. I found the key to the steel door and opened it. The victim was lying in exactly the same spot and position. I could see no movement nor hear his breathing. I found the key to the compound and went in. I looked at his face and my knees almost buckled. He looked like he had been hit by a Mack truck.

While I was telling myself not to panic, he groaned, the sweetest music I had ever heard.

The county doctor arrived and examined him. He said he would be okay. I locked him in a small cell and he slumped on the cot.

His buddy began cussing and taunting all over again. By this time I had regained my cockiness and decided to bluff him. I walked to the little cell and put my hand on my gun. I said, "You dirty sonofabitch, if you curse me one more time, I'm going to blow your brains out."

He looked me in the eyes and shook the bars. He screamed, "You're a man if you do, and a goddamn muthur-fuggin' sonofabitch if you don't."

I left in disgust.

I called the hospital to see how Two-Hat was resting. The nurse had given him a sedative and he was sleeping peacefully.

Then I called Sheriff Harris and reported the incident. I suspected his new jailer would probably mail his resignation from another city.

"Thanks, Joe, for whipping their asses," Sheriff Harris praised. "Someone needed to do it."

Working for Sheriff Harris turned out to be a great and beautiful experience. His political savvy never ceased to amaze

6

me. After I had worked for him several months, he called me into his private office one day.

"Joe, you know, I've got to run for re-election next year. As that time approaches, you will have to help me all you can. I'm very pleased with your instant popularity with the voters already. They know that you will come to them when called, and that it don't make a damn with you when or where it is, or what it's about. I swear, I wish I had half your energy. They also know that you ain't afraid of the devil, and you will take a long chance before you decide to hurt anyone." The way he was building me up, I wondered if he was trying to get me to vote for him, or if he was just practicing his politics.

"You are in for a harder time, Joe. We've got to make some changes. Two-Hat has been sick and now he's got something bad. He's got to go to the hospital and be out of work a long time. He may never work again. I'm giving you his job as chief deputy. You will get a new car and $300 a month."

"Oh, man!" I thought. "The big money at last." But chief deputy of no deputies? That's about like a groupless group leader.

He walked to the door as the girl from Social Services walked by. The sheriff's eyes glassed up and his breath quickened.

"Don't say it," I warned him.

"Boy, it's understandable why she don't bother you, Joe," he snorted. "You've just married and your little woman looks even better. I'll bet if the truth was known, you go by home every day in the early afternoon for a matinee."

"Well, sheriff, you know I wouldn't let anything interfere with my job."

"You better damn sure take good care of that little gal, Joe. If you don't, I'll fire you so you will have the time. By the way, how does she like it?"

"She loves it, boss. She's a five-star general in the war between the sexes."

His eyes glassed up again. "Well, sure wish my old lady looked that good. She ain't never seen the day she looked like your wife or that sexy gal that just passed."

What he didn't know was that my wife, Jeri, was already turning out to be as mean as a rattlesnake, especially about my planned law enforcement career that she hated.

7

OLD SILAS

Old man Silas Forseth must have been one hundred years old. When I met him, he was a night desk sergeant for the police department. He was very feeble and had to be carried to the desk from his car and back again after his shift.

His reputation was fantastic. Legend said he was a labor foreman when a local power dam was built fifty years earlier. As such he was said to have deposited more dead bodies in the wet concrete of the rising dam than the local mortician did in Central Cemetery. He rode a horse in those days and used a pick handle on the poor blacks slaving away for a few cents a day.

He was still mean as hell.

On one occasion a young policeman from another town some twenty miles away, a man whom Silas happened to like, came into the police station soaked in blood. He had arrested a circus man who had cut him to pieces with a switchblade knife.

Silas exploded! "What the hell did you do with him? Where is the sonofabitch?"

"He's out in my car unconscious," said the bloody policeman. "I didn't have my gun with me and I beat him up some with a blackjack."

Sgt. Silas yanked open a desk drawer and withdrew a large revolver. He brandished it and drew himself to his feet. "Come on, boys. I'll shoot the bastard! We can throw him in the 'cinderator.'"

"Silas, you know we can't do that, that's murder," another officer shouted.

"Murder my goddamn ass," he shouted. "He's half kilt this kid. Don't tell me I can't shoot him and throw him in the 'cinderator.' The goddamn city owns the 'cinderator,' don't it?"

He had to be physically restrained, which made him mad enough to kill us all. Silas was dangerous. When younger, he was the policeman with the proverbial weak mind and strong back. Now he had a weak mind and a weak back. But he could still pull a trigger and as long as he could do that, he would be dangerous.

Silas hated Sheriff Harris because the sheriff was a Republican. He hated two-way radios because he lacked the coordination to operate one. It was not unusual for him to try to call the sheriff on the radio and, failing to raise a reply, mumble into the radio. He would think he was on the phone to the person seeking the sheriff, "I don't know where that goddamn Republican sheriff is. If the sonabitch calls in, I'll tell him to call you," he carelessly said.

One time after such a conversation into the radio, the sheriff's voice came in loud and clear. "Go ahead, Sergeant Silas."

Silas often told about an incident that happened in 1930. One of the other officers told me Silas was an old man even then. I formed a secret personal opinion of Silas. The old bastard was too mean to die and would have to be shot on the day of judgment.

I even heard a convicted felon say once: "I don't mind being executed and going to hell, because old Silas is going to have it torn all to pieces by the time I get there and there won't be anything left."

Silas said the chief of police at Norfleet, a small town in the county, had a shootout with a three-time losing felon from Florida. The chief, after being fatally wounded, held on long enough to shoot the criminal through the chest with a .44 slug from his police revolver. The slug made a nice tunnel through an important portion of the lung complex.

The killer was turned over to Silas and his partner to transport to the State Hospital in Raleigh, one hundred miles away, in their 1929 Model-A Ford.

Silas and his partner held a caucus. "How can we kill this sonofabitch en route and make it look like an accident?"

The customary method of such an assassination is to swear the prisoner grabbed your weapon and you defended yourself. This would not work with this prisoner because he was extremely ill and unconscious.

The solution: It was January and cold as three feet up a welldigger's ass. They opened his shirt, exposing his chest to the cold wind. They rolled down all the windows. The officers wore heavy underwear, overcoats and scarves for protection. They expected the killer, with that big hole in his chest, would die with pneumonia after this exposure. If he didn't die during the trip, surely he would within a couple of days. They thought it was a good idea. It didn't work. The killer was on his feet and robust in ten days. Silas and his partner used up all their sick leave fighting a bad case of the flu.

THE .30 CALIBER DANCE

Shiny-backed scavenger flies buzzed around the blood-crusty body of Brack Montagg that was perforated by seventeen bullets from a high-powered rifle. It slouched there almost like a dummy in the dusty grass under the oak. The body reeked with alcohol. The face and head were nearly obliterated by blood and holes. A line of piss ants crawled up one leg of his soiled overalls and disappeared through a rip in his sweaty shirt near where the galluses crossed. Brack's .30 caliber rifle lay on the ground a step away.

"I'm glad Floyd went ahead and done it," I said to myself as I looked down at this carnage. "If Floyd hadn't done it, I might have had to, or someone else like me. His shooting was long overdue."

Brack was a one-horse bachelor farmer who often neglected his farming. Mostly he left the hard work to his ill-paid helper, Floyd Craven, a middle-aged black man who had been with him for over twenty years. Floyd was paid a meager salary and thought he would starve if he didn't stay with Mr. Brack.

Brack got well into a drinking spree one Saturday afternoon and this time he insisted on company. If no more suitable drinking partner came by, he ordered Floyd to join him. On that disastrous afternoon Floyd was commanded to help Brack finish the gallon jug of moonshine.

After the point of inebriation set in on Brack, he began abusing the faithful Floyd. He started shooting his .30 caliber deer rifle, blasting away at random targets around his farm. Abruptly, he decided he wanted to see Floyd dance. Without warning, he fired a shot in the ground right at the feet of Floyd, then another and another. His drunken laughter echoed around the cornfield. He reloaded several times and kept firing at the shuffling feet. Floyd was afraid to leave. He continued to high-step all over the yard until he was completely bushed, fatigued. He begged Mr. Brack to put down the rifle and leave him alone. But the pleading only further entertained Brack. He kept shooting, with every shot almost killing or seriously wounding Floyd.

Floyd became too exhausted from his dancing to dodge the bullets. That bored Brack and he stood the rifle against the oak, took a long swig from the jug and lay down on the grass for a nap.

Floyd's insides heaved in turmoil. He was frightened beyond description. Would Mr. Brack awaken and continue his game, or worse, maybe decide to shoot him in the head? Floyd thought of his seven children, ages four to twenty-two. Four of his children could look after themselves now, two worked at a sawmill and the third oldest, a girl, was about to get married. These family members ran through his reeling head. Though very poor and humble, he felt indignation and fear at such brutal treatment from a despicable man who acted like he owned his hired hand.

For about an hour he thought about it. If he left, Brack would seek him out even if he went home and undoubtedly make it worse on him. Though Brack had never before shot at him, he had subjected him to many indignities and ugly games while on these binges before. Now Floyd realized that it would never end. His hatred for Brack multiplied in his scared brain.

At noon he made his decision. Confident that Brack was safely asleep, he picked up the rifle and loaded it. His first shot splattered the brain of Brack. He died instantly. Three more shots tore into the dead man's head. All of Floyd's hatred boiled to the surface. Reloading as necessary, he riddled the body of Brack with a total of seventeen bullets from the .30 caliber rifle.

Although he was deathly afraid, Floyd now felt a little pride. He knew he would have to leave. He threw the rifle down beside the body and walked away.

About 1:00 P. M. a neighbor stopped at the home of Brack and found the body. In panic, he drove to the nearest phone and called the sheriff's office. Being the only deputy available, in fact, the only deputy, I went to the scene. After checking the body, I radioed the coroner, then I requested bloodhounds after a neighbor said she thought that Floyd had killed him and had run away on foot.

Within an hour, the coroner, the bloodhounds, two highway patrolmen and a convict trusty who worked the dogs, arrived. I had completed the usual physical examination of the crime scene. I planned to accompany the dogs.

Many neighbors, all white people, mingled at the scene. They put together a story almost ninety percent accurate. Almost everyone was glad to see Brack dead as hell. Almost without exception, they had sympathy for Floyd.

"They oughta give Floyd a medal for this...I'll help him in court, boy, I can tell what went on here...Good, I'm glad to see the

11

sonofabitch dead...Floyd oughta kilt the bastard ten years ago."

The trusty and I took up the trail with the bloodhounds, and had no trouble picking up the scent of Floyd.

It became one of the damndest chases I ever made. It was hotter than a freshly frigged sheep in a pepper patch. Even though I was young and in good condition, keeping up with the dogs proved an ordeal. We followed the trail for six hours. Through hills, fields, thickets and streams. Each time the trail went into a creek, we had to cross and find it on the other side.

Finally, in the late afternoon, we cornered the pitiful Floyd. There was very little clothing left on any of us. A bunch of shredded fabric hung on his shoulders and hips. Floyd was completely exhausted and unable to flee any more. Everyone knew that he was not a violent man, and we had no trouble taking him.

"Mr. Joe," he begged pitifully. "Don't kill me. I had to do it." He cried freely and related the events of the morning.

"Don't be afraid, Floyd," I told him. "But you will have to go to jail and you will have to be tried in court."

"Yes suh, yes suh! I knows dat, but don't let them lynch me. I got little chillun. That Mr. Brack was a mean man."

"Don't worry about being lynched, Floyd," I said. "I won't let anyone hurt you." I took Floyd to the jail and let him call a lawyer. I made sure he got a good one and I helped him make bond, unusual in a murder case.

The fusillade of bullets pumped into the body of Brack rather than the one well-placed in the head, caused Floyd the only trouble out of the deal. He served only a few months. Everyone, including me, was glad that Brack was dead.

For years I remembered to thank Floyd Craven. He may have saved me from killing a thoroughly wicked man.

GLORIA

My phone rang one morning at dawn. It was Sheriff Harris.

"Joe, I've got papers to commit an old woman from down around Coleville to the mental hospital at Butner near Durham. Stop by the jail, pick up the papers and take the old lady to the hospital."

Upon arrival at the scene around 8:30, I saw scores of people manning a tight circle around an old run down farm-house.

The closest person in the circle to the house was at least two hundred yards away. I have never seen such a group of cowardly men in my life. There must have been a hundred men and fifty women in that circle around Granny's house. All of them scared to death. Granny, I learned, was seventy-three.

As I walked through the circle, I heard whispers: "There's that new young deputy....I heard he whupped old so-and-so....he's man enough to take her if anybody is..."

Something was drastically wrong here. Any time a relative can get two licensed doctors of medicine and the clerk of court, plus the relative or custodian, to sign the necessary commitment papers, it was serious.

I walked through men of all classes. I knew some were tenant farmers while some were wealthy farmers. All hesitated out of fear and uncertainty. The old lady that I had thought would be a dull assignment turned out to be a hellion bitch who wasn't as crazy as she was mean. I walked across the porch to the single front door. I opened the door and entered. I saw an old lady in the bed and an even older lady in attendance, apparently the only other human being with guts enough to approach Granny.

Behind me the immense crowd was edging closer to the farmhouse where Granny was waiting.

I called the name of the lady I was to take to Butner and told her my name and who I was. I told her that the game was over, that she could no longer frighten people away. I was a professional officer and I would, in spite of her wishes, take her to the State Hospital.

Her reaction would have impressed the line coach of the Chicago Bears. She grabbed a quart glass milk bottle, called me an immature sonofabitch, and took a lumberjack swing at my head. I just managed to avoid contact with the bottle.

I looked back into the front yard where some of the meek people had found the nerve to come up to the porch. Abruptly I lunged out the door and grabbed the nearest two men before they could flee.

"Under the powers vested in me by His Excellency, the Governor of the State of North Carolina, through the high sheriff of this county, I do hereby duly and lawfully deputize you to help me get this old bitch into the car, so that I can rid you of the problems that have arisen because of her presence here."

Both the men attempted to flee. But my grip was firm. Everyone else dashed back to the two hundred yard perimeter.

13

I dragged the two horrified, deputized citizens into the bedroom of the old Granny. She spouted more verbal unkindness at us as we picked her up and carried her to the county car. I demanded that the crowd produce a female to accompany us on the long trip, along with the freshly recruited deputies.

A Lincoln Continental swirled up in a cloud of dust. A beautiful woman in her late twenties or early thirties got out and ran to my car.

"I'm her daughter, Gloria," she said. "What's wrong?"

I explained the situation and showed her the commitment papers. She read them and said, "Thank God. Now maybe she will get some help."

I told her it was imperative that I deputize a woman to make the long trip with me, and I preferred a relative. She said she would be happy to go.

By this time my new deputies were getting brave. Both were flashing orders to the crowd. "Stay back...don't block the road...us deputies have to do our duty..." One of them asked me if I had an extra badge. The other wanted to go by his farm and get his pistol.

Granny was positioned in the center of the back seat with one of my two new deputies on either side. Gloria jumped in the front seat with me.

We had barely cleared the yard when she slid over so close to me that driving was difficult. Soon after that, she began playing with my legs. Then she was all over me. She embarrassed me to tears. The men in the back couldn't see her hands, but they couldn't help but see how close she was sitting and how she nibbled at my right ear. During the entire trip she had her hands all over me. I think she examined by body more thoroughly than any M.D. The only thing she might have missed was my prostate gland, and she came very close to that.

I didn't know what to do or what to say, so I didn't do or say anything. She kept saying, "When we go back, I want you to take those men home first. Then you can take me home. My husband is fifty years old and he can't satisfy me."

Who in hell could, I thought. This woman obviously was a nympho. She didn't give her mother a second thought. It didn't bother her in the least that her mother was on the way to the funny farm.

Every time we stopped for gas or refreshment, she held onto me like a new bride. I was worried about the two men that I had

14

deputized. What would they think? Fortunately, both had developed an instant police complex and probably didn't give the girl or me a thought. They were offended when a motorist passed if he was ever so slightly over the speed limit. By the time the trip was over, I was convinced that both would oppose Sheriff Harris in the election.

Granny was committed smoothly. Gloria scarcely noticed her. She was too busy hanging onto me.

The return trip was even worse. She kept urging me to take the two deputies home first. I was tempted not to but her temptation was greater. So I did take the men home first. When I got Gloria home, I chickened out. Her husband was there. He came out and talked to me. He was a very nice man. His hair was as white as snow and he looked more like sixty than fifty. I don't think his age was Gloria's problem.

Next morning I reported the previous day's events to Sheriff Harris. I scolded him a little for sending me after such a bitchy old lady. "Sheriff, you know that I'm not afraid of any sonofabitch in this county, but I just can't beat up an old lady."

He wasn't even slightly interested in the old lady. In fact, he didn't even hear me. Because I had told him about Gloria.

"God, I wish I had gone instead of sending you."

I told him about her because I thought it would gain me several brownie points, stressing what will power I had and how I had upheld the integrity of the office.

Not so. He was disgusted with me. He said he should fire me for not laying Gloria. He allowed as how he surely would have. That I could easily believe.

TOP HAT BADMAN

Norfleet had two policemen, a Monday through Saturday chief, and a Sunday officer.

As the deputy-less chief deputy, I patrolled this little town and all other rural areas on the weekends. On one such visit, I was hailed by the Sunday officer, Macie Birdle. He waved four warrants, signed by the mayor, for the arrest of June Cleary, an immense black man of fearsome reputation. Now he was free on bond for murder and everyone in Norfleet and vicinity was scared to death of him except Chief Dancer, who was off duty at that time.

I asked Birdle for the details.

15

He had stopped several blacks in a car that morning for driving recklessly and drunkenly on the streets of Norfleet. When he approached the car, June Cleary jumped out, flashed an eight-inch switchblade, and snarled, "No white sonofabitch is gonna arrest me. I'll cut your heart out."

I asked Birdle what he did about the .38 on his hip. He told me he didn't even think of it. "What did you do then?" I asked.

"I ran," he admitted.

"You left your car?" I asked in disbelief. "And with a .38 pistol on your belt?"

"I'm afraid so," he said.

"Okay, where is this guy?"

"He's over at the Top Hat," replied Birdle. This was a notorious hangout in the black community.

In that instant, in my heart, I committed murder. My plan was to go into the Top Hat Club, single him out, and kill him. And at the time, it wouldn't have bothered me too much.

"I hate to tell you this, Joe, but I just can't go in there with you," Birdle told me.

"You mean to tell me, you are gonna let me go in that hell hole place alone?"

"I can't help it," he moaned. "I just don't have the guts."

"Okay, you bastard, but I want your badge tomorrow. If something bad happens to me, you better tell the goddamn truth, and if there is any reason for it, call an ambulance for help or anything that a good officer would think of. If you hear some gunshots, don't haul ass, do your duty. Because in all probability that sonofabitch will tell me the same thing he told you on the square. If he does, he's a dead nigger."

I left Birdle in the car. So help me, he was trembling like a leaf. I entered the infamous Top Hat Club, which for years had been taboo to all white people. There were at least two dozen blacks in there. Most of them were nursing a Saturday night hangover. I announced my identity for the record and called for June Cleary.

A big man, probably six-four and 230 pounds, arose from an old couch. "I'm June Cleary, What the hell do you want?"

"Mr. Cleary, I have four warrants for your arrest." Tensely, I waited, poised. I had come into this place to kill him. Because I just knew that he would reach for that knife. But some instinct must have warned him. He never put his hand close to his pocket.

16

Instead, he snarled, "Why you little bastard, you know I'm not about to go anywhur wid you."

Quickly I tried a smoking left hook to the big nerve across the jaw bone of his face. He moved enough that the blow landed high on his cheekbone. Blood gushed all over his face. The blow knocked him down. Seconds later, he jumped to his feet and took a sidewinder swing at my head. He missed and left himself wide open. I caught him with a good right uppercut to the left side of his chin. He went down and out.

I quickly looked around for fear of an ice pick entering my body between the shoulders. But no one moved. June started reviving. His eyes opened whitely, then his eyeballs moved back in place. "June, do you want any more, or are you going peacefully?" I asked him.

"I go anywhur you say, suh," he said.

I jerked him to his feet, pushed him through the crowd and kicked him in the seat of the pants every few steps. At the front door, I kicked him out onto the ground at the edge of the street. I took another look at the crowd. They seemed to appreciate this dethroning of the king of all local bad men. Obviously he had had all the fight he wanted. I made a lot of black friends that day. He had his neighbors scared half to death and had constantly intimidated all of them.

Officer Birdle still waited in the parking lot, his hands, lower lip and voice trembling like a whipped child. I put the prisoner in the back seat and sat beside him while Birdle drove. Before we got to the main road, I asked him where the knife was that he was going to cut officer Birdle's heart out with.

"I've got it in my pocket. I'll give it to you," he said.

"No, better not," I said.

"Why not?" he asked.

"Because, you sonofabitch, I'm hoping that somewhere during this ten-mile trip to jail you will get up enough courage to pull that knife on me so that I can blow your goddamn brains out. I'm not satisfied with you."

Cleary immediately threw both hands on the back of the front seat and left them there throughout the trip. When we got to the jail, I was amused at a black trusty who knew Cleary and who noticed the blood all over him. I overheard Cleary tell the trusty: "Well, man, you knows I's the best boxer around. But that little white sonofabitch, Joe Louis-ed me a while ago. His left hand is like lightning. I never saw it, but baby, I sho' felt it. I

17

believe he can whup anybody!"

Just luck, I thought. The big bastard could have broken my back had he whammed me with one paw.

Cleary never gave any other officer an iota of trouble. He became a law-abiding citizen. Never again did Norfleet policemen have to dread facing this dangerous giant in such a precarious situation.

After this incident, I told officer Birdle that he would resign as an officer of the law or else. He asked what I meant. I said if he continued to wear the badge of an officer and the uniform of the town, I would personally kick his ass, tear off his badge and turn it in to the town clerk. He never worked another day as a policeman

CHAPTER 2
THE MEN FROM ATF

Two men who strode into the sheriff's office that day were from the ATF, a federal agency specializing in criminal investigation of moonshining. It was an elite outfit that I already knew about. I had a secret ambition to become one of them if the opportunity ever arose.

The younger man, about my age, was very friendly and sharp. The other man, in his fifties, was not sharp. He was nervous in his work from his age and health, as I learned later. They had a joint investigation going with the sheriff about a moonshine still.

Sheriff Harris and I accompanied the federal men to raid a copper pot moonshine distillery in the Republican stronghold of Lublock township. The younger agent, Clarence Heather, captured my imagination quickly. He proved to be a true professional. And professionalism in law enforcement was something I dreamed of, seldom found and never really expected. I ramrodded my job in my own way, always expecting some sort of fatal cave-in any day. But it never happened.

Clarence became an instant idol. By the time we returned from our raid, I had made a decision to go after the ATF as a career. If the ATF produced professionals like Clarence, then the ATF and I were on a merger course. Get out of my way everybody!

Two weeks later, Clarence returned to our city. I candidly hit him with my desire to become a treasury agent. His first question was, "Where did you finish college?"

"The only college I have ever saw was Wake Forest, on my way to fetch a prisoner from Rocky Mount, North Carolina," I confessed to him.

"Well, that's not the only way. If you are intelligent enough to pass the Civil Service exam, with three years of specialized experience in investigation, you have a chance."

I went to Salisbury, North Carolina, in January, 1955, and took the Civil Service exam. Boy was it loaded! I have never seen

19

such monstrosities for a human being to answer. The examiner told us that only one of twenty passed it. And he was talking about college graduates.

I endured the four-hour agony and was later informed that I had passed with a score of 80. It was then up to me to prove that I had three or more years in criminal investigations. With the help of Sheriff Harris, we compiled enough propaganda to make me look like J. Edgar, Jr.

However, the sheriff was quite unhappy about my seeking employment with the U. S. Treasury. He said, "Joe, I'm only going to be sheriff four more years. Then you are a cinch to run and be elected. My God, these people in this county love you to death. You could beat me right now."

"Sheriff," I said, "I've got some sad news for you. You are not going to be sheriff for four more years. Little Bob is going to beat your ass so bad that you will not believe it." Little Bob was very popular as a game warden, and even more popular as the son of a former sheriff, the grandson of a former sheriff, and the second cousin of a former sheriff. All of them named Bob.

"Joe, I don't know why you think that," Sheriff Harris said. "I beat Malley Lowerly by 1,700 votes."

"Sheriff, this time you ain't running against Malley. You are running against Little Bob and he's going to tear you to little pieces."

My prediction proved correct in November. Little Bob beat Sheriff Harris by about 1,200 votes. The sheriff told me, "If you hadn't warned me in advance, I would never have believed it."

We were to remain in office until January. In October we had to police a Negro camp meeting at a community church about fifteen miles from the county seat. Every year the black people had this camp meeting on the third weekend in October.

Sheriff Harris told me I could expect nothing but trouble all day long. Two-Hat was sick and couldn't help me. The sheriff didn't work on Sunday on account of his religion, unless he just had to. So I worked alone, as usual.

That rickety old wooden church leaned whichever way the wind blew. You could throw cats through the cracks in the walls. Several days before the fateful Sunday, people flocked in from everywhere. I saw Cadillacs from California, New Jersey and from all over. They put up carnival sideshows and concession stands. They even made and sold snowballs.

I went to the scene alone, wearing a Colt .45 with a six-inch

20

barrel. The weapon was an old World War I revolver that looked fierce; I wore it for psychological reasons. The first thing I noticed were two little black boys, about six years old, who ran alongside me and eyeballed the gun. "Just look at that muther-fugger," one of them said. Black people have peculiar attitudes about guns. They are not afraid of an ordinary blue revolver. But they are scared to death of a pearl-handled or a nickel-plated gun.

I locked up fourteen carloads of people that day. The only reason I didn't lock up more was because I didn't have time. Those people would go into the church, inhale all kinds of old time religion, then go outside, buy a drink of moonshine, frig in the broomsage field adjacent to the church, shoot craps, cut each other up, and raise all kinds of hell. Then they would go back into the church and praise the Lord.

I found it necessary to arrest a black woman who was getting too much out of line. I had to fight my way through the crowd to get to her. Then I had to fight my way out of the crowd to take her in. On the fifteen-mile trip, she cussed me to every SOB in the book. I gritted my teeth and restrained my temper. What I really wanted to do was slap hell out of her. But I endured the abuse and delivered her to the county calaboose unmarked and intact.

I took her into the jail lobby. Floyd, the new jailer and my real friend, was on duty. He was a monster, weighing about two hundred fifty pounds, as I said before, and he was mean enough to do his job well.

The black bitch started her cussing of all law enforcement officers and especially abused Floyd. After all the patience I had practiced, I was going to tell Sheriff Harris to gain more brownie points.

Floyd slapped her a good fifteen feet. The first time she said an uncomplimentary word, that big man creamed her, and good.

I thought. "If that ain't a hell of a note. I let that bitch cuss me all the way to town and I am a great gentleman and won't lift a finger. After all my politeness, Floyd knocks her on her ass."

My acceptance into the ATF came. I was offered a job as a criminal investigator in North Wilkesboro, North Carolina. I went to Charlotte and met the wheel of all ATF agents in our state. His name was Nick.

Without a doubt, he was the most dedicated and hardnosed officer I have ever seen. He briefed me in short, ragged terms. He already knew all about me, he was that professional.

"What are you going to do about your military position?" he asked.

I was a First Lieutenant in the U. S. Army Reserve, having obtained a "Sears-Roebuck" commission by correspondence courses. I didn't know how to answer him.

"Get out," he said bluntly, "You don't have time to fool with the army."

I thought to myself. "What the hell have I gotten myself into?" But Nick turned out to be a great man. Later in my career I was accused of being just like him. I considered that a great compliment.

I still had to go through an oral interview. So I went to Atlanta to face several men comprising a panel, each man represented a branch of the government service.

The ATF executive on the panel turned out to be Hercules DeLoops, the big wheel of enforcement for the outfit east of the Mississippi River. They called him Herk for short. He was brilliant and very knowledgeable about the technology of ATF operations.

He was a prima donna with an emotional and ego problem. He expected subordinates to bow down to him. It took me several years to realize this. I suspect the base of his problem was outside the office.

Herk was vindictive and used the process of associations to ruin careers. Nick was too popular and strong for Herk to crucify easily. So it became a war oriented to the associations of people with Nick. He could have very well expended his talents on something of more importance, like putting the big bootleggers in jail.

He carried out a vendetta against Ray Ervin, Nick's best friend. Ray was a saint, one of the most respected men I ever knew. Ray was married to a living doll named Liz, an artist and perfectionist in music, painting, decorating, and homemaking.

If you were friendly with Ray, you were crosswise with Herk. I committed that great sin. Ray was my friend and I didn't give a darn what Herk thought about it.

The postman brought the news. I had been selected and assigned to North Wilkesboro, the Moonshine Capital of the World. Nick had to be responsible for this. He had been a group leader there himself. He thought I was a good prospect. He had pegged me as a hard charger, figuring I would work many overtime hours and give it all I had. He was right.

THE WILKESBORO BUNCH

The federal ATF office in North Wilkesboro occupied a dank portion of the basement in the federal building so elaborately constructed many years before during a Republican administration. This county enjoyed a Republican Rock of Gibraltar status in a staunchly Democratic state.

I reported to a dark, tattooed agent of about forty, who was acting group leader in the absence of the sho' 'nuf group leader, Jonathan East, the latter being on his honeymoon with his second wife.

This temporary boss, Roy Shortsir, could have substituted well for George Allen. Devastatingly funny behind a most serious countenance, he never laughed at his own jokes.

After introducing me to the crew, Roy took me to the pistol range, where I was not allowed to wear arms for Uncle Sam without being qualified with a .38 revolver.

I fired away at the targets, missing each shot. I blamed the gun and tried again. Roy said, "My God, man, you couldn't hit a bull in the ass with a bass fiddle. I thought you had been an officer about five years already."

"I have," I told him, "but I've never used my gun."

He opened the trunk of the government car and took out a double-barreled, sawed-off shotgun. "Try your luck with this."

I knew I could handle the shotgun. I fired both barrels at once, jolted by the damndest recoil I have ever experienced. But the buckshot mutilated the target. I was in. Roy gave me a sharpshooter score.

Back at the office, all ten of the guys wanted to meet the fresh meat. I sized them all up shortly and spotted at least two genuine characters.

One was the ageless and famous Carlton Fine, a legend in his own time, having earned the title "Dean of all Revenuers."

The other was a rangy man of about forty known as Bilge Butler. A renowned country witticist, Bilge was the son of an old time sheriff in an even more mountainous county. He never tired of telling stories of his father.

Sheriff Butler locked up a lady prisoner one night. Next morning, she banged her tin breakfast plate against the bars and raised hell.

"Sheriff Butler, come up here and get this seventy-five cents and go get me a box of Kotex, please," she pleaded.

23

"Kotex, hell," the old sheriff replied. "You can eat oatmeal like the rest of the prisoners."

•••••

Sunrise next day found Bilge, an agent named Bill Coolege and me in a surplus military jeep that must have gone ashore in the Normandy invasion. There was no back seat and I had to sit on a box of some sort. We careened around dirt road mountain curves that would have been scary as hell to walk on. Coolege drove. He had the misfortune of being cross-eyed. One eye stared solidly on the road and the other directly over a cliff, at times a thousand feet high.

"Bill, by God, if you're going to drive where you're looking, let me have the wheel," Bilge complained.

I started examining the interior of the jeep. Finally, my eyes settled on the box on which I sat. There were large red letters on two sides. D-**Y-N-A-M-I-T-E.** Good God, I thought! What sort of a crew have I tangled with? The box bounced all over the rear seat area all day, with me on top of it. I didn't say a word, but I don't recall needing a laxative for the next eighteen months.

•••••

Carlton Fine was our only living convert from the prohibition era. He remembered when there was so much graft in federal agencies that you had to wear a badge to keep from bribing one another. He also told about how you had to be a slick politician to get any kind of promotion.

I worked with Carlton for many months. He trained me well in woodcraft, creeping and crawling, surveillance and how to wriggle through several strands of barbed wire without ripping your balls out. One of the best lessons I learned, however, I learned quite easily by myself. That is, never, **NEVER** piss on an electric fence. Not even if you live a hundred years.

One pitch black night, Carlton, an agent called Smitty and I found a large moonshine still in full operation. A moonshine distillery normally is raided in one manner, but not necessarily all the time. That method is silently surrounding three sides, and having a "flush" man approach from the fourth side. He gets as close as possible, picks the most advantageous moment, and on a pre-arranged signal, grabs the first man he can get and shouts directions of flight of the others.

24

This time, Smitty and I had to cover all we could of three sides, while Carlton did the flushing. He always served as flush man because he knew every bootlegger in the county by name, rank and serial number. He could identify anyone that he could see. He could also creep and crawl through the infield of Yankee Stadium during a series game without being seen.

While waiting on Carlton fo flush, I heard the two men working at the still talking. One said, "Hurry up, Alfred, and let's go. We're through."

In a whimsical voice, his partner said, "Wait a minute, I'm going over to this here telephone tree and call goddamn ole Carlton Fine. Ding-ling-ling. Come on and get me, Carlton, you old bastard. We're fixin' to leave."

The next voice I heard was that of Carlton. "Okay, Alfred, I got your message."

I heard a loud scream as Carlton must have grabbed him by the seat of the pants.

Later, Alfred said, "Damn quick service if you ask me."

The other man tore through the brush toward me. He sounded like a stampeding horse. I tackled him and went up in the air, then down. I turned a flashlight into his face as I sat on top of him. His cocked right arm and hand held a large-bladed knife pointed at me only inches away.

"Put that knife down carefully, friend," I warned him.

"What knife?" he asked.

I tapped his right wrist. He looked around, saw the knife and said, "My Gawd! I hope you didn't think that I wuz gonna stab you! I was caulking cracks in the cooler box with this thing. I shore appreciate you not shootin' me. You ever need a favor from me, buddy, you got it." He was amazed.

"If you really want to do me a favor, stop pissing on my legs," I told him.

•••••

Wilkes County proved exciting every day. It could very well have been a little nation of its own. The people were above average in honesty and integrity except for the business of moonshine. Almost everyone was, or had been, associated with the liquor business. It was a traditional way of life.

These mountain people didn't resent an officer of the law too much as long as he played fair. Many times I arrested people

25

at a distillery, a felony charge, and due to convenience of the government or the defendant, I have released them after proper identification, and instructed them to be in the office of the U. S. Commissioner at a certain time on a specific date. Without exception, I always found such a defendant there on time. They were honor bound.

The greatest mistake an officer can make there is to acquire even the slightest reputation for lying or exaggerating when a defendant is on trial. To them, lying makes that officer a blue ribbon sonofabitch, unworthy of living any longer.

To these proud people, making moonshine is not immoral. It's an offense to the U. S. Government, but they don't worry about that since most of them think the guv'ment makes liquor too. They say the only difference is in the tax. Besides that, many of them think the guv'ment makes it chemically, putting foreign ingredients in it, making it quite unsanitary. A favorite competitive remark is, "Damned ole guv'ment whiskey ain't no good. You can't see through it. Moonshine has no color, it looks like clear water."

Of course, the U. S. government does not manufacture whiskey, but it exercises tighter control over the legal manufacture at the giant commercial distilleries in this country than over any other industry. Agents are assigned full time to supervise these distilleries as to quantity, quality, proof, etc. I have a friend, now an enforcement agent, who served as a storekeeper-gauger for many, many years. This is part of his Treasury Department job but not an enforcement position. I have known him for about fifteen years and have never seen him drink alcohol. Once I saw him offered a drink which he turned down with the remark, "I can't drink, I'm an alcoholic." He swore that when he was a storekeeper-gauger at a large legal distillery, while proofing whiskey each day, that he drank a quart per day for seven years. Naturally, he was drunk for seven years.

When I first went to Wilkes there was little industry except illicit moonshining. It had its share of politicians, churches and an abundance of very good people. But you just couldn't get across to these people the wrongness of making booze. It was a legendary vocation for hundreds of mountain people. No officer is worth any more than his sources of information. In this county, good information was difficult to come by. On the other hand, some county officers, preachers, and practically everybody often hampered our intelligence-gathering processes. A paradox became apparent. The honest county sheriff would get information on a moonshine still and then, depending on the politics of the informant, he would weigh the problem. He left destroying stills to our agency. If the informant was a big politician who could screw up the next election, the sheriff had to be cautious. But his information was generally accurate when he passed it on to us. The sheriff's understanding with federal agents went like this: "We have dozens of moonshiners in this county, but catching them and destroying stills is the work of the ATF. I'll have enough to do carrying out my other duties." He handled the report of a felony as if he were an agent for a foreign country and was engaging in high treason. He did his duty but carefully guarded his actions. If he had done differently, he would not have lasted as the county sheriff. It proved good business for us. His information was accurate and saved us a lot of time.

So the Great State of Wilkes, for the enforcement of federal moonshine laws, belonged to a dedicated little group of ATF Investigators assigned to the place. Assignment there, to some, meant Siberia. Others immediately fell in love with it. But we had something in common. Our off time and social activity was largely within our own group.

This system had great advantages. What assistance the sheriff did give us was great. We still had the professional North Carolina Highway Patrol in emergencies. Thankfully, we had no prima donna who thought he owned the land on which we were charged with enforcing the laws.

A county-wide ABC election campaign was being waged in Wilkesboro when I arrived. Most people were indignant to think that one of those old ABC stores might locate in their county. Damned old chemical government whiskey that you couldn't see through.

Odell Jolson, the long-time bootlegger of tax paid whiskey (not moonshine), was recognized for twenty years as the "red liquor king." He ran a whorehouse on the side and sold bonded liquor by the drink, pint or tractor-trailer load for massive profits. Most people in Wilkes, even the moonshiners, did not drink their own product. They made it to sell, not to drink. Consequently, most of them, and other drinkers, bought bonded booze from Odell.

During the heat of the ABC campaign, a television newsman from Charlotte visited Wilkesboro and on live TV interviewed

27

people concerning their attitudes about the election. By pure chance, the TV man stopped Jolson. He gave his name to the TV man, who asked: "Well, Mr. Jolson, as a long-time merchant of this area with diversified business interests, what is your opinion of the ABC vote situation here?"

"Horrible, horrible!" Odell replied. "It would be a most terrible influence on our young people and I'm strongly against it." He failed to mention his vested interest.

Not long after that interview, I led a raid on a moonshine still in the Windy Gap mountains nearby where I found 5,003 (that's right, five thousand and three) bottles of bonded, tax paid booze, evidently stored there until Odell could "influence" some of those young people.

As usual, the Wets lost the election, making the good Christian people rejoice. Now that there would be no drinking, the bootleggers exulted, because they could stay in business. The Bible-totin' hypocrites were happy so they could still play games with their families, business associates, and shoot the preacher a line of crap about how happy they were to see the ABC stores voted out. In the meantime, school buildings, already condemned and about to fall down,would have to be made do to educate little children who didn't have a chance.

•••••

Jonathan East, the regular group leader for Wilkesboro, returned from his honeymoon. He looked a little pale and ear lobe thin. I had heard much about him.

He had begun his career with the U. S. Army Military Police at Fort Bragg where he served as sergeant during the Big War. Thereafter, he entered the Treasury through the Bureau of Narcotics, which at that time was a part of the U. S. Treasury. There he spent a year, transferring to the ATF which pushed him all the way to the top, having crowned his career at fifty as the chief of enforcement in the entire United States.

When I met him, most of this was yet to come. He was working on it, however, and the keenness of his ambition manifested in a multitude of ways. He was considered the number one agent in North Carolina and he worked like hell to make everyone believe it. In addition, he was the greatest PR man and politician that I have ever seen. As the years rolled by, he took on all the hopefuls in Atlanta, Washington or anywhere else who got in his way. It became an absorbing study in human

28

nature. One by one, supervisors who had been taken by Jonathan with ease, suddenly realized the truth. Jonathan was after his job, or one higher. The supervisor immediately got a bellyful of him, only to discover it was just too damn late to cut him back. Always several jumps ahead, Jonathan had the higher bosses thinking he was Jesus Christ.

I had training problems with him for awhile, and at one time, formed the idea that he was a tyrannical bastard who should be thrown off a cliff on an appropriate raid. My chief resentment was my mistaken impression that his religious conversion and holier-than-thou conduct was a part of his game. I later learned such was not the case. To this day, he strongly holds to his Christian principles.

In my judgment, in watching Jonathan's progress, and how the self-styled Sharpies fell before his advance like sheep to the slaughter, I believe him to be a near genius. He did not have a college education, but in a short time he worked from the bottom to the very tip-top, the ATF counterpart to J. Edgar Hoover. He has my admiration and respect.

CUSSIN' GEORGE

"Cussin'" George Fowler was a mean and shrewd major violator of the U. S. liquor laws. He had operated for thirty years and was one of those experienced shiners who, once in a while, had the guts to shoot the works, that is, put up a giant outfit in a not-so-unobvious location and gamble that he could operate for a month or two, thereby setting up a profit of about $50,000 for the venture.

In this case, he installed it in his backyard chicken house. He had operated little more than a week when the All-American ATF fullback, D. C. Lumus, found it with his keen sense of smell. Agent Lumus quickly organized a raid, including a federal search warrant for the premises. It became one of my first experiences in this category.

A work of engineering and plumbing art, this distillery was powered by four homemade coke-burning boilers, and consisted of about 15,000 gallons of mash, the fermenting ingredient which is cooked off to produce the alcohol. It was a mass of material, completely filling the large chicken house. Cussin' George didn't bother to pump water from a nearby creek, but elected to connect a hose to his household water supply, a well

29

beside the back porch. We surprised George in the act.

"D. C. Lumus, you sonofabitch!" exploded George. "You are the goddamnest still-finding officer I have ever saw. You're stationed in Winston-Salem, anyway. What the hell are you doing over here? I'd rather see that goddamn government airplane come here than you. Your goddamn nose is too big. How you gonna get that mess out of my chicken house without messing up my whole place?"

"Why didn't you ask yourself that question before you put this big outfit in here, George?" Lumus asked him.

George's question stimulated an important issue to be resolved. How **were** we going to do this? Hand by hand, piece by piece was the gentlemanly way and, in fact, the only way prescribed by the manual in the case of contraband within a building. However, this would take two full days of hard labor, to say nothing of the terrible physical toll taken on the destroyers. More importantly, it would consume the valuable time of four active agents who might otherwise discover and destroy several other large outfits. It quickly grew to a matter of national security. The revenue of the country had to be protected at all costs and it could not be properly done if four active agents were confined to a two-day job of toting out Cussin' George's outfit after slashing each piece with an axe.

The decision: Dynamite the distillery. If George's chicken house went up with it, then he could always complain and make a claim against the government. There was no hope of survival of his chicken house if the appropriate amount of TNT was used to eradicate the distillery. Besides, the house had never seen a chicken anyway.

No amount of George's cussin' would stop us. We did show much compassion by not blowing up his well, which was very much a part of the violation, even if it did furnish his household. We compromised and busted up his pump with an axe.

About forty charges, eight of them double strength, destroyed the chicken house and loosened a few boards on the back of George's dwelling. Our patriotism resulted in four agents being free after only two hours' work, to pursue others engaged in defrauding the United States.

For many months when we passed George's house, he would yell foul names at us. But I cannot recall George having another moonshine still adjacent to, nor even in the same neighborhood of, his dwelling.

CHAPTER 3
THE BREEDING GROUND

This mountainous environment in and around Wilkes was the breeding ground for many of the world's most famous stock car race drivers. Most of the young male offspring of the big-time moonshiners built and drove very powerful cars. By the late 1950's, they developed machines that would run 150 mph plus. But this was a secondary part of their development. All such cars were primarily designed to transport moonshine into the market-place—Winston-Salem, Greensboro, Charlotte, Richmond, Philadelphia, even New York City, or any other place where it could be promptly exchanged for cash.

These people practiced driving as a full time job. Most of them were capable of making ninety-degree turns at 100 mph, or, in the case of a few, 180-degree turns and head right back at you.

My first experience with one such driver proved embarrassing as hell. Imagine the U. S. government providing us with little gas-saving Mickey Mouse cars to chase these speed masters with!

I jumped a new booze buggy one moonlit night. My foot rammed into the carburetor as I determined to stay with him. It was like sending a one-legged man to an ass-kicking. The guy played cat and mouse with me for thirty minutes until I was getting the idea that he was not so great and that he just might not escape.

Then he got bored with the game. We hit Highway 321 about ten miles west of the city on a long straightaway. Suddenly he appeared to turn on a large rocket. His taillights pulled away from me at an incredible rate. He went down the road about two miles and made one of those "Thunder Road" 180-degree turns and came right back at me—on my side of the road!

Here he came, hell-bustin'! He wanted to play chicken. I played with him. But I was the chicken. I got the hell off the road and banged down a large embankment, having to employ a

31

wrecker to retrieve the disgusting example of automotive crap the government forced me to drive.

"I'll get you yet, you pile-driving bastard, or one of your brethren," I vowed to myself as I listened to his rocketing engine fading miles away.

Soon, I would find a way to total or "accidentally" burn the government's automotive absurdity assigned to me. Then I would go after one of those sweet bellowing babies that I had just chased so ignominiously. Do it through the laws of seizure, confiscation and forfeiture.

There was an unwritten code in ATF hierarchy. If you were smart enough to catch a "hot" car, get it forfeited through the courts, ATF would ask for it to be converted to government use and assigned to the apprehender.

This sounded like a good deal. But the trick was how in hell were you going to catch a 150-mph car with the mechanical miscarriage car of government issue? Especially when the 150-mph driver could out drive half the race drivers in the country, anyway?

Other ways existed, though not so effective and much more dangerous. All types of roadblocks had been devised and used. On most occasions the master drivers in their fearsome machines would run any roadblock successfully. Many times I have seen them knock hell out of as many as three crosswise automobiles filling a road, hit one side and tear up the concrete getting away.

We always shot down the tires, but even a .44 magnum would not immediately immobilize a tire. The air lasted sufficiently for the driver to get far enough away to hide. The .357 or .44 magnum would demolish the engine if properly hit. But you're defeating your own purpose because that beautiful engine is the prize you're after.

We had very little luck with burning high octane gasoline on the highway (which the State Highway Department frowned on) to scare the driver into bailing out and abandoning the car. They were too cool. They simply called on the machine for more speed. It looked like the circus bit where the lion jumps through the burning ring.

One highly effective investigative aid was the "whammy," consisting of three twelve-foot lengths of one-inch flat iron hinged together to complete road width when unfolded. Four-inch, razor-sharp spikes were welded each two inches from one end to the other. The instrument could not be seen in the dark with ordinary headlights. It provided for no cars on approach to alarm the driver. Cars were then dispersed at about three hundred-yard intervals on the other side of the whammy. When a car hit this gimmick with all four tires, supporting two thousand pounds of moonshine, all the tires immediately went limp. The car could not possibly continue.

The big trouble with it, however, was an embarrassing fatality rate among shine runners. Too many times, the cars would turn end over end, burst into flames and, on a few such occasions, kill the driver. This was very bad, it being highly illegal, anyway. And it required too many goddamn government forms to be filled out. Even worse was the loss of the dream car.

Such accidents prompted many of our supervisors to frown on using the whammy as well as the old accepted method of shooting the tires down. The immediate result was the ordeal of having to fill out all those forms. Eventually, we were ordered to cease use of the whammy and firearms in pursuit or in any other situation except to save life. Some eager bastard probably with a master's degree in accounting, somewhere up the line, even caused us ultimately to fill out a form each time we discharged a firearm.

I couldn't help wondering what old Silas would have said about this.

•••••

Fate sometimes fills in the gaps in unexplainable ways. One of the world's most famous race drivers had been born and reared in Wilkes. His driving genius had been developed from early teens behind the wheel of a whiskey car. At this particular time, he was all over the national race circuit and was internationally famous. However, his legal residence was with his relatives in this area.

We had reports that he was still involved in illegal alcohol on a brokerage basis, having long ago risen above latent involvement with it.

We had located a monster moonshine still on the race driver's father's farm. Jonathan led a raiding party to it on a dark, wet and cold night. We approached on foot from the back way, across a complex of mountains I thought competed with the Alps. Jonathan and I had found the still and checked the mash the day before. We were certain it would be in operation this night and

33

that we could catch the operators. But because of an all-day rain, the fermentation had slowed and the thing sat there in the wet woods. We had no choice but to stake it out until the next day.

Never have I been colder. All our clothes were saturated. I even went to the still and found some old sacks to wrap around my body to help me withstand the numbing cold.

Just a little before daylight, we were rewarded. Oh, how we were rewarded! Three men came to the distillery with a large wagon load of half-gallon glass jars to hold the day's run of whiskey. We could not see who they were. Two other agents and I were ordered by Jonathan to assume positions on the east side, while he would flush from the west.

While waiting on Jonathan's shout, I heard voices and the scraping noise of a coal scoop used shoveling coke into the furnaces. Any minute now all hell would bust loose and only God knew what would happen.

I heard Jonathan's warning identification. Then he yelled in unbelievable surprise the name of Mr. FAMOUS RACE DRIVER himself!

Then Jonathan yelled, "No...FAMOUS RACE DRIVER...no, don't hit me with that shovel!"

WHAPP! I hard the smack of the scoop and assumed that Jonathan was out of the action.

Three men hauled ass out the east side and entered the pasture near me. I picked out the one that I thought was Mr. Big. I don't know how he did it, because he was a very large man, but he passed the others like they were in reverse. I chased him several hundred yards.

"Oh God, if that's who I think it is, steady my feet and strengthen my lungs until I catch him," I prayed.

I nailed him just as we hit the fence. We tore three strands of barbed wire from six posts we slammed into it so hard. We both went sprawling. I sprang up first.

FAMOUS RACE DRIVER recovered and crouched into a boxing position, his right fist cocked, his face strained in disbelief.

"Be my guest, FAMOUS RACE DRIVER, if that's the way you want it," I said. "Fighting's my specialty."

He stared at me a few seconds, then relaxed. "Don't believe I'll take the chance," he said.

We were both cut up pretty badly and bloody from the wire. After some first aid, I questioned him. "Why are you out here?"

34

"One of the boys was sick this morning," was the only reply he made.

But man, was he sick! He had an incredible reputation he had earned all over the world. I felt sorry for him because of this. But he was the biggest catch since Capone. And I really basked in the glory of it. But to see this man working at a moonshine still was like seeing General MacArthur on KP.

Once he surrendered, FAMOUS RACE DRIVER proved very cooperative, if rather silent. He even helped us bust up his still.

Next morning, headlines in the sports section of *The Charlotte Observer* blared: "Nationally Famous Race Driver Caught at Moonshine Still."

I got a little sick for him, thinking about the terrible embarrassment that it must have been. The federal judge didn't act sick, though, a few weeks later, when he sentenced him to three years in prison. He actually served a major portion of that sentence with time off for good behavior.

•••••

My patience and determination paid off. I seized **two** new Pontiacs in a combination roadblock, running roadblock, shotgun ambush and bridge blocking. We caught a top major violator, a member of the notorious Taylor syndicate. All hell broke loose that night. An indelible night to remember. He never knew what hit him until we swarmed all over him.

Nothing on the Wilkes roads ran and roared quite like a whiskey car, and we could hear him coming miles away as he left the valley and started climbing the winding road. We were poised and ready. Tennessee Charlie, our lookout and spotter man, confirmed it by radio, saying he was loaded and barreling. There were no turn-offs. He had to hit us.

Then he blasted around the curve and the seconds seemed to tick by in slow motion.

Hell, there were two of them running in convoy! Two!

Follow-the-leader, they plowed into our roadblock full tilt, knocking hell out of the vehicles.

Then big name syndicate driver opened his door to bail out, but he looked directly into the bore of a deadly .44 held by "Ears" Edwards, who would have shot holes through him in a wink had he reached for a gun. The other driver was no problem.

After the collision, we figured the roadblock junker car was worth only $5.00. But we had two $6,000 liquor cars with the sweetest engines I have ever seen even though there was several hundred dollars damage to the Pontiacs caused by our over-eager junker driver. Both cars were forfeited shortly by the courts and assigned to our post in accordance with our unwritten code.

I babied the one assigned to me fantastically as to maintenance. I began practicing high speed driving on dangerous mountain curves. It wasn't long until I thought I was ready to try the ninety-degree turn at 100 mph plus. Before I became too proficient, I took up a few trees, gas pumps and utility poles. I did not have time to really master the maneuver until I had to use it one night to save my life.

According to enemy intelligence reports the secret of the ninety degree turn at 100 mph plus goes like this.

If your turn will be to the right, try to judge your distance to your turning place at about 350 feet (varying with road surface, construction, elevation, even wind velocity) and turn hard to the right. The car will not, or should not, turn over, but rather, go into a sideways skid toward your objective. Then, about two seconds prior to reaching the side road, put the accelerator to the floor and hold it there. If your judgment and actions are correct, you should then be on your way.

Dick Torre and I had some rather good information that one of our most colorful and skilled shine runners would make a trip to Charlotte on this particular night in a new Olds coupe with a tri-power Pontiac engine in it, exactly like the engine in my government car. The trip was reportedly arranged for about one a. m. over U. S. Highway 2.

We found a good ambush position on a turn-off about fifteen miles north of Charlotte and assumed our position after nine p. m.

With nothing much to do until one a. m., we reminisced a good deal. Dick had some good experiences to share with me. We generally agreed on which judges and attorneys were son-sofbitches. We told a few war stories and government service tales.

Dick said the most embarrassing spectacle of his life was the time he and a partner arrested an eighty-year-old woman, the sole occupant of an old farmhouse. A bootlegger had paid her a few lousy bucks to use her house as a stash place.

There was a provision in the federal rules of criminal procedure for a "consent" search. This meant that after fully advising a suspect of his or her constitutional rights, in that if he or she refused consent, that the officers could then enter with a valid search warrant that was extremely hard to obtain.

Dick and Bob knew the liquor was there, so they entered, pushing by the old lady, searched for, found and seized over 300 gallons of booze. Since no one else was present and since there was no evidence against anyone else, Dick and Bob arrested the old woman.

Dick said he later noticed that the woman said absolutely nothing on the way to the U. S. Commissioner, nor did she say anything at her arraignment. However, at her trial in U. S. District Court, she had a prominent local lawyer. The officers testified they carefully warned her of her rights and that she stated that she fully understood those rights. Thereafter, they alleged that she told them to go ahead and search. So much for the government's case.

But her attorney introduced a sister, also in her eighties, along with four neighbors. All of them proceeded to testify, under oath, that the defendant had never in her life heard a sound or spoken a word of any kind. She had been a deaf mute since birth. A motion by the defense for a directed verdict of acquittal was promptly favored.

Dick and Bob took the royal ass-chewing of a lifetime by the federal judge, who never tried another criminal case based on a consent search.

•••••

The weather was chilly enough to freeze the outside moisture on the windows and windshield and interfere with identifying passing cars. We had waited since midnight. At 2:10 a. m., I saw the form of a coupe pass. We talked about the possibility that this was a moonshine hauler for a few seconds while the coupe floated around a curve half a mile away.

"What the hell are we talking for, there's nothing like taking a look," I snapped and we were off like a rocket.

When we reached the curve, I saw the cutting on and off of the coupe's tail lights over a mile away. The driver had spooked when he saw us and had really poured it on. Now he was running by moonlight with lights out, except when he approached intersections.

I put the accelerator to the floor. Shortly Dick said, "Damn, you're doing 135."

At that instant, I saw the on-and-off flicker of the tail lights on a side road to my right. A ninety-degree turn! I whirled the wheel. My coach had been right. The car didn't turn over, but I was much too far to make the turn. We must have skidded 300 feet by it. Then I hit the brakes and whirled the car again. Now I was getting close to the 180-degree turn at 100 mph plus. I'm glad we had no audience, because that turn, though somewhat successful, must have looked terribly awkward. But this time, I hit the side road.

The fugitive was still running without lights except for the intersections. The dirt road, unfamiliar to me, made a wide, sweeping turn to the left. As I went into the turn, he was coming out the other side, a distance of about two-thirds of a mile. I saw his headlights flick off and on. They shone on a large state road sign which said STOP. I immediately assumed it was a crossroad as the headlights of his car went off again and I thought he went straight.

We came boiling over the hill, and our lights hit the sign. Instead of a crossroad, it was a T-intersection. Down our way to about the end of the road on which we were traveling, some 200 feet away, loomed the damndest big state-built barricade I have ever seen.

I remembered it takes 350 feet to skid properly in the 90 degree turn at 100 mph plus. Here we had only 200 feet at something like 120 mph plus.

I gave it a good college try to the right. The Pontiac skidded by the right road with enough force and speed to skid across the ditch, eat up the thirty-foot grass median, and splintered the large barricade into toothpicks. This barricade consisted of a twelve-inch pole horizontally across the top.

Fortunately, no metal lodged against the wheels. Both headlights were gone and half the windshield. But the engine still ran. "If that bastard can run without lights, so can we," I growled. Our radiator was busted, so I yanked off the fan belt, then checked to see if Dick was hurt, then we were off.

We picked him up first by the roar of his engine. Apparently he was lost, also, and penned up in a small town. After some foolish chances with the roads and his crippled car, we were close on him. We let him have considerable powder and lead, some of which struck the car, but none hitting him or the tires. The duel went on in and out of streets, unknown to both fugitive and pursuers.

Finally, he roared onto a little dirt road that we had not been on. Down a hill he zoomed at at least 80 mph. From a block behind, we saw him hit the steel cable that was across the road to the city landfill.

The cable cut the roof completely off the hardtop coupe, making an instant convertible out of it. And it missed the driver's head by about an inch. He didn't even get glass in his eye.

He bailed out and left the booze with us.

We discovered this driver was very lucky. There were four bullet holes in the rear of the car, two at exact shoulder blade height. The booze stacked up in the rear saved him from the bullets.

Uninjured, he quickly disappeared in the darkness. But his luck ran out when we called the local sheriff who happened to train bloodhounds for a hobby. The dogs picked up the fresh trail and we caught him before daylight. His skill and guts were typical for the locality.

We got no kick out of the news, two weeks later, that another pair of officers had jumped him in another city with another good car loaded with booze. This time his luck really went sour. He was killed in a flaming roadblock. I always wondered, but never asked, What kind of roadblock? The whammy, maybe?

•••••

It was not the artistic, poetically inclined people, or the overly intellectual type that emerged from college and took up the ATF cross to bear for a living. The few who escaped Big Herk's screening machinery did not last long for many reasons. One couldn't stand such dangerous work, or working all night. Others couldn't stand the sight of blood, particularly their own. And all those who let the wife wear the pants didn't last long. Those who stayed and enjoyed doing a good job would have made excellent guerillas in some South American revolution.

We had to be tough, strong, half-mean, and had to do many of the same acts that the criminals we were catching did. Most new agents had to live the identical life the moonshiners did. He had to make whiskey, buy it, drink it like a man, and drive hot cars loaded to the gills to the large cities. About the only difference in the undercover agent and the criminal was that the criminal didn't have to make notes to later aid him in filling out all those goddamn government forms required.

My first personal problem to arise out of ATF employment was the violent reaction of my wife, Jeri. She raised hell about my job all the time and used it as fuel to feed the flames of wrath kindled in her the day of her birth. My adverse contribution to the marriage was that I loved my work too much, and was not hung up on domestic life anyway. I probably never should have married.

My obsession with ATF began to change my nature away from the rigid training and environment of my childhood. My home county was a conservative island of Southern Baptists, drys, hard work and little programmed entertainment. My mother was a living Saint who lived for her people, friends, and most explicitly, her Primitive Baptist Church. To this day, the Primitive Baptists have no budget, no collections, and no salary for the minister. They are as devout as Catholics and live their religion. They still have annual ceremonies in which they humbly wash each other's feet.

In my home area, the most devastating criticism about a person was a whispered, "He drinks!" It was from this background that I entered ATF. I was violently opposed to legal or illegal sale of alcohol, and hated it with a purple passion. Gambling was just as bad.

The storms of my career have blown me far off course from this conviction. In a few short years I departed from all of these things in practice. My new friends were soon kind enough to teach me to play poker. Everywhere they drank. In bars, in the woods, in automobiles, and most actively in hotel and motel rooms after duty in court or on special assignment away from home. I politely refused to join them for a while. But as I became more and more hooked on my work, and my trust and my dependency grew with these fine friends, I realized that for all their evil ways, they were honest, hard-working and dedicated men to whom my life was entrusted many times. They gambled and drank but it did not make them any less good than the most proper deacon in the church.

And too, the only easy way to endure constant drinking parties, is to join them. So join them I did. In my particular case, the first drink was a serious mistake. I believe that I was born with a drive to excel in everything I do. And drinking was no exception.

40

CHAPTER 4
TWO DIRTY HATS FLOATED IN THE RIVER

My first promotion came quickly. In less than two years, I was promoted and sent, as group leader, to a large coastal port city, headquarters for a seven-county area. In each of these counties there was a thriving major illegal alcohol manufacturing industry that was a problem. However, the investigative and managerial staff I inherited was a bigger problem than the bootleggers. Every one of the current assignees was transferred to the winds.

I started with a clean slate—one veteran with two months' service and three brand new men. They were all college boys, but they couldn't use a typewriter. In those days, each agent typed all of the numerous, though unnecessary, goddamn government reports.

The departing crew members were so involved in choosing sides with various politically oriented local enforcement agencies, each opposing the other, that they brought only one lousy defendant to court during the preceding six months.

At the next term of U. S. Court, we boasted of 199 defendants in spite of our strangeness to the area and the indifference of local officers.

My predecessor, in briefing me on the situation prior to his departure, told me of a community, overwhelmingly black, that was good for one large distillery per month. "However," he pointed out, "You will never arrest anyone there, their grapevine is too good."

He should never have said that. He had no way of knowing what a challenge he presented to me.

Accepting that challenge resulted in the death of three men, the near lynching of our whole local force, permanently eliminated the good-for-a-still-a-month syndrome, not to mention a three time effort by a law enforcement officer in one of the counties to have me indicted for murder by the State Grand Jury.

We received our first report of the distillery in early April, about a month after my transfer to the post. The informant gave me a detailed map of its location on the shore of the Cape Fear River and reported it to be a huge operation.

My preliminary investigation included research with the

41

USOA, ASCS involving the use of aerial photos, the U. S. Army Corps of Engineers as to accessibility, and I was determined to keep our information and strategy absolutely secret from the sheriff's office. This was for several reasons, the most prominent one being our reports from honest officers and credible informers that some members of the sheriff's department were crooked. If it had been a matter of worrying only about the sheriff, however, the problem would not have been so serious, because he was too damned inexperienced to make a successful crook. We had reliable information that he had approached some of the bootleggers in the county boldly demanding payola for protection. They reportedly called him a stupid sonofabitch, and some allegedly told him that he was too dumb to catch them, so why pay him?

Never forgetting what my predecessor had said about "You will never arrest anyone..." we set out with grim determination to counter that prediction. We amassed all the equipment and supplies deemed necessary, and set out on foot about dark for the distillery with a raiding party of five men. Particular attention was given to snake bite kits for each man since this was all swamp country crawling with copperheads, cottonmouths, and rattlers.

Our trek must have been at least seven miles. Undoubtedly the most miserable seven miles put together in the USA. How we did it from the backside of the river, I'll never quite understand. There was more than a 50/50 chance we would get lost in this wilderness, with no landmarks known to us, and thus become the objects of search and rescue by the U. S. Coast Guard. But this didn't happen. Dead tired, we hit the distillery right on the nose about 4 a. m.!

The informant was right. This was a monster—a big steam outfit with many thousands of gallons of prime mash. Luck kept smiling upon us. In all probability the distillery would be operated that day.

With another agent, I reconnoitered the total perimeter. Our effort indicated that the distillery was being worked from the river by boats. There were no inland trails. I made a note of this in drawing up a raiding plan.

The distillery was situated about 75 yards from the main boat landing. Our plan included the assignment of each man to a position and an area to cover, after which we withdrew to await appearance of the operators.

By reputation, this operation was different from the norm.

It was reportedly run by a local syndicate that had three investors. Each got a third of the profits. The scope of the operation earned each of them a place on the major violator list maintained by the ATF for the seven Southern states comprising the moonshine belt.

The list normally contained twenty names, in order of importance and size, and was our counterpart to the FBI's ten most wanted men. These three men were all black. There was only one other black man on the list.

In the first light of dawn, I made a quick examination of the distillery and noted from its condition that everything was intact. It was so big that it was literally a daily operation. We had received the information twenty-four hours earlier and the operation had continued after our preliminary preparations. To me this meant that the allegedly crooked local sheriff and his deputies had no knowledge of our having the information.

It was difficult for me to keep that kind of officer out of my mind. To me a corrupt, greedy law enforcement officer should be hung.

We only worked one investigation with the bastard. That was when a large violator muscled in on the local bootleggers. The sheriff and his chief deputy set them up and insisted on helping us in the execution of the raid.

Information in that case was very accurate. Four men came to a wooded area in two trucks loaded with several hundred gallons of booze. There were six officers participating, four federal agents and the sheriff along with his chief deputy. We had a big fight in the dark and arrested the four men.

The opportunity was golden. In the dark, one of my enterprising agents beat the living hell out of the sheriff by "mistake." He looked terrible and wound up with two broken ribs. I complimented the agent later on his accident.

"That was no damn accident," he whooped. "I've been wanting to whip that sonofabitch for months. This way he will never know for sure that it wasn't an accident." He suspected it, though, I learned later.

Just after dawn, three black men came to the distillery in a small boat and began preparing it for operation. They worked about an hour and it looked as if no one else would come to assist them. As the "flush" man, I ran into the midst of the three, grabbed one and directed two other agents in on the others who fled.

At the exact same time I let my presence be known, another boat bearing four more black men, including the three major violators who owned the operation, glided into the landing. Our contingency planning was good. The agents jumped the men the moment the bow of the boat touched the landing.

Three of them jumped in the river, knocking another into the water. The latter drowned immediately.

The remaining three were desperately trying to swim to the opposite shore and safety, fully clothed and with boots on. I pleaded with them to return, but to no avail.

An agent, born and reared on the beach and an expert swimmer, dived, fully clothed, into the water and began pursuit. I could see that the black men were losing strength before they were halfway across.

I fired two shots over the head of the one nearest me and he turned around, and tried to get back. We fished him out of the water with a long pole. The other two were exhausted. Both started sinking and begged for help.

John, the agent in the water, tried to save one, but the man locked an arm around his neck and pulled him under. I thought John would never come back to the surface. When he did surface, he was in trouble, and was dragged back under. Frantically trying to get John in the boat, I no longer cared about the violators, but I was scared as hell that we were going to lose John.

Finally, he managed to get his head above the water and breathed again. I fired a shot near him to get his attention and yelled, "John, if you don't turn that bastard loose I'm going to shoot you!"

He had managed to break the strangle hold that the bootlegger had on him, and made a feeble effort to meet me in the boat. Seconds later, he hung on the side of the boat and we got him on board.

I quickly looked back at the others. The one John had his ordeal with was already dead on the bottom. The other one was pleading for help in a strangled voice. Then he was gone also. Only two old felt hats floated as if someone had flung them into the river.

John was the only agent who had offered pursuit by jumping in the river, and he had almost lost his life. His act became a desperate and heroic effort to save the poor men. No one could have swum to them after they got in trouble, in time to help them. John got to them only because his first intention was to catch one of them. I felt extremely helpless because I couldn't swim across a good-sized bath tub. In addition, the water was cold and had a powerful undercurrent.

We were at least five miles from civilization. My first thought was to find a phone and call a rescue squad. Perhaps if I could run fast enough and find help close enough, we could revive them. I started running the direction my instinct told me was toward the nearest highway. I knew that I had two chances, slim and none.

I covered the several miles in the shortest time I have ever covered a like distance on foot. Thank God, I thought, for my luck or judgment in finding the highway.

I stopped a car and ordered the driver to take me to the nearest phone. I called an emergency operator and asked for a rescue squad. The operator informed me that there were no rescue squads in the area. I asked for the U. S. Coast Guard, that was located at a further distance. They would send two men for dragging operations. Then I called the N. C. Highway Patrol and asked for emergency assistance as I had a real apprehension in my mind about what would happen once the word got around about the drownings.

Then I called Nick, my boss, in Charlotte. His voice was calm. In fact, it was cold and matter-of-fact.

"Are any of our boys dead?"

"No sir."

"Very good. Are any of the three drowned violators on the major list?"

"Yes sir, all of them, sir."

"Good!" He was elated. His voice grew excited. He had a terrible obsession against major violators. To him they were enemies just the same as if we were at war. The death or capture of a major violator to him was the same as the death or capture of a general officer in warfare. He was that serious.

"Were any of them black?"

"Yes sir, all of them."

"That's bad. That means twice as many goddamn government reports."

"Look, Nick, I'm sorry, but I can't talk any more. I've got to get back to see about the boys. God only knows what will happen down there before we clear this up."

I led the Coast Guard dragging crew to the scene. Already

the blacks were gathering. I was desperately concerned, partially because I felt that the local sheriff would never provide us with help regardless of what kind of emergency arose.

The whole day turned out to be one horrendous emergency. Knowing now what we endured throughout that day makes me wonder why any of us are still living.

That river water was so cold and had such a strong undercurrent, the bodies did not sink and rest in the same position. It took the Coast Guard team all day to retrieve them. Two sheriff's deputies arrived and began sympathizing with the already ugly crowd.

We estimated the number of black people that gathered on the shore that day at about 5,000. The only white people were the Coast Guard crew, the coroner, who was no friend of ours, and the four of us.

Rumors began flying.

The federal men had murdered the Negroes by shooting them and throwing them in the river. This rumor intensified throughout the day as the crowd grew larger. With our backs to the same water that claimed three lives, and almost got two more, we had no chance with this angry mob. It was really a mob.

The damned coroner took the first body retrieved, and then the later ones, and cut every piece of clothing from it and examined every inch of the body for bullet holes right in the presence of this angry mob.

I was the only one who did any shooting, and I knew I didn't hit anyone. But Lord! I was sweating out the possibility of a hole having been made by the grappling hooks. Fortunately, there was none. To this day I'm sure that four agents owe their lives to this coincidence.

I swore that if I ever got the chance, I'd fix that damn dumb ass coroner.

Three or more agitators began working up the mob fever. Open threats of lynching were thrown around.

I went from one of the agents to the other, trying to keep them calm, remembering that they were all brand new and green as hell. They all came through. No one ever acted any more professional and cool—with one exception.

This was a South Carolina boy who was emerging in his training as a real character. He was big and strong, but didn't have enough common sense, in the beginning, to pour piss out of a boot with directions printed on the heel. He was very intelligent though, and learned rapidly. I had already decided that we would have a problem at times until he seasoned, because he was the type who did something instantly even if it was wrong.

He was not only unafraid of this mob, he was actually cocky. In the presence of everyone, he singled out and collared one of the principal agitators and said aloud: "Look, you black sonofabitch, there are three of them bastards out there dead now, and the next goddamn time you open your mouth, SPLASH, you're Number Four!"

The hair on my neck stood up. "My God, this may do it," I shuddered. But nothing happened.

I evaluated the situation and came up with only one possible chance that we could survive this ordeal. The solution was was to keep constantly aware of the positions of the few agitators. My plan was, in the tragic event this mob tried to lynch us, to quickly kill the leaders, the mouthy ones working up the mob fever, in the slim hope that this would stop the others.

I walked around the front edges of the mob, ignoring all kinds of verbal abuse and picked out the five biggest troublemakers and looked them over good. The worst one claimed to be a nephew of one of the drowned bootleggers. Then I assigned four others to an agent for possible shooting, and picked the worst one for myself.

One apiece, I thought, hoping that the thousands remaining would be shocked enough to stop. I told my boys not to hesitate or wait too long, but rather shoot to kill the instant as many as two of them put hands on either of us.

In my brief report of this incident to the highway patrol and to the boss, I didn't realize that this situation would be so grave. The patrol never arrived at the river, but I'm sure they didn't realize that the lives of four officers were in such critical danger. Later I learned that they were fully occupied handling the heavy traffic into the area off the main highway.

The deputies stayed about fifteen minutes and didn't return. There was no route of retreat or escape, so my plan may not have been a good one, but at least it was an attempt. Besides that, I believe that any man, if cornered and about to die would find solace in the feeling that he is going to take at least part of his adversaries with him.

The coroner finished the examination of the last body in the late afternoon and found no holes. That fact and the cool manner with which we handled the situation made it begin to look like we might survive. I found the mob weary and quieting down so I gave them a speech.

I assured them that the shots fired were only to shock the men already half dead into enough mind to return to shore, that no one was shot at, and that every effort had been made to save them. I expressed my genuine sorrow for their deaths and then explained that a full investigation by our agency and others would show that we had acted honorably.

I still believe that the fourth man in the water would be dead had it not been for the gunfire.

The crowd began to melt away. Threats of future retaliation were left with us. But by this time the danger seemed to have passed. There was quite a reaction.

I heard that the NAACP had investigators at the scene that afternoon. If this is true, I'm impressed with their fairness, because we never read a word or got any criticism from that organization for the conduct of our investigation and handling of this tragedy.

Subsequently, I had several reports that the mental midget sheriff appeared before a Superior Court Grand Jury on this occasion and attempted to get me indicted for murder, but failed. The sheriff had no knowledge of the meaning of evidence.

•••••

Violent law enforcement in this area had been known before, according to bits of a story told by local officers. It was alleged that local ABC officers, with only city authority, chased a bootlegger by automobile from the city across one of the long bridges that was a part of the highway complex. There had been much gunfire, presumably at the fleeing man's tires. One of the bullets had hit the man between the ears and killed him. Violators reported that the officers discovered what had happened, and then deliberately ran over the man's head, mutilating it so badly that it could not be determined if he had been killed in a crash or by a bullet.

I cannot speak for the veracity of this report, but I can state that never again were these enforcement officers (who were far above average for this locality) allowed to leave the city limits to enforce the laws under any circumstances.

This is similar to a defensive tactic of some officers who carry a "dropper" everywhere they go. A dropper is an old hand gun that cannot be traced. If in the course of his duties, the officer makes a mistake and kills a criminal, thinking of course, that the man had a weapon but finding that he did not, he drops the "dropper" on the body, thereby making it a case of justifiable homicide. This has worked on many occasions. The trick is, don't let the same dropper show up in court in too many cases, and don't forget it and leave it at home (as happened in one case) and have someone find the clean corpse before you can get back with the dropper.

Red was an eager beaver who didn't know the meaning of fear. He began his short career on the first day with the ATF acting like a twenty-year veteran. He would tackle anything, usually for a while taking the wrong course of action. He had been a salesman while working his way through school, and a good one. Consequently, he was also a con man, being very persuasive in many ways, the ways depending on with whom he was dealing.

He moved to the city to take his job and rented a house on the beach, ten miles away. Driving to work on his very first day, Red got arrested for speeding by a city policeman, but then arrested the policeman for interfering. Red was very proud of his first case. Then I told him that not only did he have no case but that the policeman might sue him for false arrest.

Disappointed, Red then defended himself in state court in a two hour trial. The judge forthwith found him guilty and fined him fifty dollars. The average fine for fifty-five in a thirty-five zone was twenty-five dollars. Red began to look like something special.

I knew if his guts and energy could be harnessed, he would be outstanding. While trying to help him polish off the wire edges, I developed my first gray hairs, which, as my work with him continued, were quickly followed by many others.

I still wonder why he, the other agents, or I survived all the stunts he pulled off. I distinctly remember one occasion in which a constable in a distant county had information that an old Ford would deliver a load of booze across the state line from South Carolina at about midnight on a Wednesday . At that time, although every other federal agency and every state organization had modern FM radios, we had none. The reason was that our national chief of enforcement was a stupid little bastard who had retired from the military and in trying to run the ATF, thought he was Patton back at the Bulge. He refused to buy any radios for the whole nation except for a certain Mickey Mouse brand manufactured on the West Coast. Everyone tried to

49

straighten him out and away from this inferior brand and more specifically from AM to FM. He wouldn't listen.

Once at a big conference where he looked for support after becoming sensitive to the subject, he asked for examples of favorable field use of his pet walkie-talkie radios. I raised my hand and got the floor.

He smiled and said, "Ye-s-s-s-s, now here is a very active man. Please tell us about your use of the talkie radio."

"Yes Sir," I said, "I used mine to kill a goddamn rattle-snake." And I sat down.

He raised hell. He jumped all over my boss and later threatened to have me examined by a head shrinker. It was interesting to note that a few years later he retired to a small West Coast town where the radios were manufactured.

Red and I drove an old government pickup truck the seventy-five miles to meet the constable. He told us that the liquor car would come up a certain dirt road at about midnight, and that it would be occupied by a black man or two. We made our plans around the absence of radios. I placed the constable in his personal car and Red on a point within horn blowing distance down the road. I concealed the pickup about half a mile away. The plan was that when they saw the car pass, they would fall in behind without trying to stop him and thus avoid endangering the constable's family car. The signal was three short blasts on the horn. I was then to block the one lane road while they moved up from behind.

Midnight passed. About half-asleep at 1:30 a. m., I jerked awake, not by a horn blast, but by six rapid shots from a .38. A car fitting the general description of the liquor car came toward me at full speed, too dangerous to block. I fell in behind him. He led a lively chase.

Several miles up the road the driver suddenly swerved into a man's yard, crashed through his septic tank and wrecked his car pretty badly. I jumped out, immediately hearing loud spewing of air escaping the left rear tire. I had a chill when I saw a bullet hole at exact shoulder blade height. I feared the very worst.

All four doors flung open and a variety of different black women, small children and one old man poured out of the car. I quickly looked inside to see if it contained someone who could not get out.

My heart almost stopped beating. A big fat woman slumped

50

in the front seat. I just knew she was dead.

I put my hand on her shoulder and she lifted her head. Then I saw a cute little baby hungrily sucking on a nipple. She smiled the sweetest smile I ever saw.

The man of the house came out on his porch and raised hell, threatening to shoot us all. When he saw what had happened to his septic tank, he really raised hell. Red and the constable drove up. Red was holstering his .38 with a proud grin on his face like he had just won the Masters.

I winked at him and said, "Did you see that bunch of KKK members in that big Chrysler who just shot up these fine folks?"

Red caught on and said, "Yes sir, they went like a bat outta hell toward South Carolina."

"Let's go!" I yelled. We took off. Down the road, I stopped and tried to thank God for letting us off the hook again.

"For God's sake, Red, don't ever shoot at a tire in the dark on an uneven road like that, at that speed," I pleaded.

Red looked offended. "Tire, hell! I was shooting at that goddamn nigger under the steering wheel." Hitting the tire had been an accident.

Back in the office at about 11 a. m., the sheriff of that county, one of our few friends in the area, put in an emergency call to me. He wouldn't talk on the phone and told me that he must meet with me immediately.

The sheriff was very upset. The black family that we had shot up were good people and hard-working farmers. They share-cropped with a big white farmer to whom they promptly reported the incident. He was a big shot local politician who suddenly decided he was Sherlock Holmes. He dug the .38 bullet out of the upholstery and turned it over to the sheriff, demanding an investigation including ballistics examination and comparison with bullets fired from the guns of "that goddamn wild bunch of federal men who worked that area."

I had to admit to myself that the bastard had a good analytical mind, at least. The bullet would be perfect for comparison, having no blemishes on it.

I candidly reported to the sheriff exactly what had happened. He said, "Well, that sonofabitch helped me win the election and he's over-bearing as hell, but we can't stand this kind of evidence." He threw the bullet into a large mass of honeysuckle vines. Along with it went the only chance of any real evidence and embarrassment to the government.

51

It caused me to remember again that the name of the game with an officer who will take the risks that he must to be a good one is: "I DENIES **THE ALLEGATIONS AND DAMNS THE ALLEGATORS.**"

This will only work, however, when there are no bullets to compare with those fired from his gun.

Red and I had a report of the existence of a moonshine distillery in a certain section of one of our counties known as "Revenooer Creek." And it made our fearless guts quiver.

This community got its reputation many years ago as a result of the cold-blooded murder of two ATF agents who entered the community, situated on a peninsula with only one road through its center, meaning you had to come back out the same way you went in.

All of the residents, extremely clannish, were involved in the moonshine business, and we had no friends there.

The two ill-fated agents went into the midst of the community and destroyed a small distillery that didn't amount to a hill of beans revenue wise. They didn't even arrest anyone, as it was unattended and no evidence existed for an arrest. On leaving, they passed by the houses along the only road. There was a very small creek that crossed the sand road about a half mile from the relative safety of a public road.

This creek was easily fordable, but required slowing down to prevent splashing water on the engine and drowning it out. As they almost stopped in the middle of the creek, rifle shots burst out from both sides of the road and both died instantly.

An extensive investigation finally resulted in the conviction of a father and son for first degree murder. The case was made without the slightest bit of assistance from the local populace. The father and son ultimately died in the North Carolina electric chair in Raleigh.

This capital punishment was not accepted by the already militant and clannish group, and it became very dangerous for any officer to enter this road where the two agents died in the ambush.

All of the stills ever seized here were what we called "kickover," and unworthy of the time and effort to find and destroy from a revenue point of view. A kickover is a very small distillery that might just as well be kicked over or destroyed. It was not worth an expensive investigation.

Perhaps this fact and the natural apprehension of officers

52

to meddle with these people brought on a rationalization that the place was taboo. Nevertheless, information occasionally came in on violations there, and Red and I could not ignore them.

A show of force with two or three agents in each of two or three cars was the safe way to do it because the people were going to see whoever entered, regardless. But my logic was that you just don't take four or six men to do a two man job. Doing so is admitting that it's a dangerous undertaking. I didn't like to admit to these moonshiners that they had our number and we were running scared.

Red and I went in alone about dawn. Tension gripped us, especially when slowing down to cross Revenooer Creek. It made you get a tight grip on the seat cushion with your buttocks and it made the hair prickle on the back of your neck. After crossing without incident, Red said, "Well, we made it."

"We're going in, Red, not coming out," I reminded him. "The last two guys made it going in, you know."

We went all the way to the end of the road, passing many hostile onlookers and ramshackled shacks. "Mean looking bunch of sonsofbitches," I thought.

Our information was not specific. The only way to cover the whole area was to walk behind every house on the west side of the road, as the creek was the only source of water and it lay on the west, running parallel to the road and the fatal crossing, some two miles back the way we had come.

I had Red crop me out and told him to go all the way back to safety and to give me two hours to work out all the possibilities on foot, then to come back and pick me up two hundred yards short of the creek crossing.

I got out beyond the very last house, walked around the edge of a swamp and toward the creek. I dropped into a ravine. As I got to the lower part of the swamp, I heard a pop and zing. About four inches over my head a twig popped off its branch and landed on my shoulder. A .22 rifle probably.

I hit the ground just as a stacatto of shots burst out, all of the bullets hitting brush and branches two or three feet over my head. I almost dug a foxhole with my nose. Repeatedly, I tried to gain my feet and get a look, but I was pinned down in one miserable position. It sounded like the bastard was firing one of those sixteen-shot, semi-automatic rifles, the kind that will shoot as fast as you pull the trigger.

Helpless in this position, I counted every shot for something like an hour. Then I decided that this rifleman could keep reloaded and firing till doomsday and that I had to think of something.

The swamp edge ran about one foot lower than his shooting level, making that one foot safe for the distance of the swamp, perhaps three hundred yards to the end of the deadend road, where I had entered.

Using my nose for a plow, I painfully worked my way toward the road. It seemed an eternity passed. The .22's still zinged into my old position. Finally, I got to the road. From there I could see a man standing on the back door stoop of a shanty, rapidly shooting into the spot where I had first been a near miss. Apparently he had not seen me leave and he thought I was still in the swamp, either dead or pinned down.

I crawled through a field of broomsedge in a semi-circle until, it seemed like hours later, I came to the front of his house. It was one of those shotgun affairs, having a hall down the middle to the back porch. Now I could see the back of the man. He still fired away. By the time I nailed him, I had counted 72 shots he had fired at me.

I crawled to the front door and eased into the hallway. Then I made a headlong rush. Before he could hear me and turn and fire point blank, I tackled him from the rear. We went sailing off the porch onto the ground about eight feet away.

He begged and begged for his life. He said, "Hope God may kill me, mister, I didn't know you was in that swamp. Oh, please, man, please have mercy on me!" I hadn't said a word about being in the swamp.

He was three sheets in the wind and could hardly stand erect. Take him in and book him for assault on a federal officer, I thought to myself.

My better judgment told me that I had no real way to prove that he actually knew that I was in the swamp, and besides, the federal judge in our district didn't give a damn if a bootlegger did shoot at one or two of our boys.

I decided to take a "roadside nol-pros" and work him over. I took the rifle from him and wrapped it around a tree. I let him feel the true fury of my nickname "Joltin' Joe." When I finished with him, he was pitiful. I hit him on the point of the chin with an uppercut that broke the jawbone hinges on both sides. His teeth were sparse and somewhat realigned. I don't know if he had any broken ribs, but I left them in terrible condition. Neighbors poured into the yard. I gave one of them $20 and told him to call an ambulance. Not a word was uttered. The man took the $20.

I was about an hour late getting back to Red who asked what the devil had happened. When I told him, I had to take the wheel from him to keep him from going back to the community and starting trouble all over again.

Never again did we have any trouble from Revenooer Creek.

Duty in this coastal town was a dream. About the time I started getting designs on permanent residence, Nick had other plans for me.

He called me one morning about five o'clock, customary for him, and told me to be in Charlotte at nine o'clock for an urgent conference about some undercover work. This meant money. It was extremely difficult to get money in those times for any ATF operation. I felt complimented that Nick had chosen my post for money for undercover work.

The IRS, under which we worked, although they collected billions, at times were grounded. I can remember the time when we were instructed to stop driving a government car for any reason. No purchases for anything. This of course, paralyzed us. It was ridiculous and absolutely false economy. Just another stupid predicament some little analyst in Washington decreed. This condition has been known to go on for weeks and weeks. Your network of informants and intelligence dissolves and the damage is massive and near permanent.

I walked into Nick's office and shook hands. As usual, he got right down to business. But I jumped the gun, asking how much money I could get.

"Money? For what?"

I reminded him about the undercover work he had mentioned on the phone.

"Forget the money," he said. "I told you that so you would get here in a hurry and not raid some little old nickel ass still before you came."

He paced a few seconds, then went on. "I've got a real personnel problem at another post, also a coastal city, that I believe only you can handle. I've got a group leader there who was born there, grew up there, and went on the job there, and hasn't been anywhere else. He has never worked with anyone but a bunch of ABC officers, deputies, policemen, all of whom are very clannish. In fact, they will try to hang you before you get started. The leader is not worth the powder it would take to blow him to

55

hell. He hasn't been off his ass in fifteen years. Neither has he had any desire to learn anything. Right now he couldn't catch the clapp in a nigger whorehouse. Another big problem, Joe, he's going to stay there and work under you."

"For Pete's sake, Nick, why don't you transfer him to Rome, Georgia, or something?" I asked.

"I'd sure as hell do it, but this is a deal with him and the goddamn local politicians. He voluntarily steps down if we leave him put there."

This was a real blow. Give up the beautiful city that I was getting hooked on. Leave Red and the other recruits who were developing so well under me. The men at the new post were unknown to me and I quite frankly dreaded the assignment. But duty is not to be put aside.

As soon as I arrived there in the fall, my worst fears were realized. I had one man who was friendly, a Duke graduate, who was a fire breathing guy more motivated to cut the throats that were cutting his than catching moonshiners. He filled me in on everyone, and spent considerable time telling me how inefficient the former leader was and what a colossal group of SOB's were the local police, sheriff's department, and most assuredly the local ABC enforcement nuts. The latter consisted of two men, one being a phenomenal man in his sixties who was a very good agent in the peak of good health and able to compete with any man in hand-to-hand combat. With the exception of him, I learned that my only friendly cohort was absolutely right.

These officers made no bones about the fact that they would rather see a criminal go free than see me make a case against him. They would not work with me, conspired against me, set traps for me, including the bait that is supposed to catch everyone—namely, sex. I don't know why they didn't nail me with that technique, but I eluded them.

Without informers, local officer assistance, and even basic communication, it seemed like an impossible task. However, never one to be put down, I went to Charlotte and had a serious talk with Nick. I told him this problem was in his lap, that I had to have some money for undercover work. He agreed to go all out. We imported a professional undercover agent, not government, and set him up as a bootlegger. Right away, the police department, ABC force and sheriff's department declared war on him. I had informed them of his activities for legal purposes, so that anything they could catch him for would not be valid.

The whole bunch of bastards started harassing him. He was stopped sometimes fifteen times a day, cursed, abused and threatened. Luckily they never caught him with contraband. We began switching government cars on them, and had a total of six before the project was finished.

The ABC chief, the prima donna sonofabitch who acted as quarterback, was very frustrated. Our man began making contacts and was soon buying whiskey from many violators, and better still, he hauled large loads from the manufacturers.

The chief couldn't stand it. He had to talk to me. He came to my office on the third floor of the U. S. post office. His voice had acid in it.

"I've got three things to say to you and nothing more. First, your boss in Charlotte is a first class sonofabitch. Next, I'm king of law enforcement in this town and if you play ball here at all, it'll be on my ball field. Last, I'm going to catch that goddamn bootlegging undercover man of yours and seize that government car."

"Is that all?" I asked.

"That's it," he rasped.

"Okay," I said. "As to playing ball, you play on your field, and I'll play on mine. I don't need you. Next, if you catch the undercover man and seize the government car, I'll arrest your ass for interfering with a federal investigation, since I have already formally and legally advised you what he is doing. Last, you have cursed my boss, which I can't take, and I'll give you one minute to get your fat lazy ass out of my office or you will find out how it feels to float down three stories without a parachute."

He left in a rage.

All through this crisis, the former group leader did nothing. He did nothing against me, nothing for me. He just did nothing. He sat back and smiled at my misery.

It came to a climax after we wound up the undercover investigation and took about thirty defendants to federal court. The ABC chief went to the defense counsel and convinced them he would like to testify against me and the undercover man.

The trial was hectic. The ABC chief did testify and stated under oath that this city had no liquor problem until I came there with the undercover agent and "went into the liquor business." He was almost jailed by the federal judge and he was permanently barred from any appearance thereafter in any federal court in that district.

57

We had a big personnel conference in which Nick gave the former group leader hell for not helping me in this situation.

He said, "But, Nick, I've been here fifteen years and I've never done anything wrong."

"You're partly right, " Nick retorted. "You've been here fifteen years and you have never done anything, period."

Conditions were better on the surface after this. The government was paying four men to man this post and I was the only one who would speak to any of the others.

AIRBORNE

A wilder and more courageous bunch of bastards never existed than the men of the U. S. Coast Guard at the time I worked in eastern North Carolina. At that time, the Coast Guard was part of the U. S. Treasury Department and we regularly used their aircraft and pilots for surveillance, search and destroy missions and other uses. They were half renegades like ATF personnel. They worked hard and played hard. Some enlisted men were pilots then, unlike the other services.

Their craft was always something that the Navy or Air Force had obsoleted years ago. But they flew the hell out of them. Many times the skill of these pilots caused criminals to be caught. Other times they caused near heart failure to the ATF observer who always accompanied the pilot on each mission.

The commanding officer of a large Coast Guard station assigned a tall, good-looking chief petty officer to me for a flight. Complete strangers, we walked to the big plane and he acted a little worried.

"How do you get in this goddamn thing?" he asked.

I couldn't believe my ears. "Uh...uh...up that ladder, I suppose," I quavered.

He climbed up to the cockpit and looked inside. "Hey...good God! Look at all these gadgets! Do you know how to start it?" His voice sounded concerned.

"No, and I don't want to learn," I said. "I just remembered I've got an appointment with the veterinarian about my pet elephant." I started back down my side. He laughed uproariously and I knew everything was all right.

We took off in that thing and he was a complete master with not a flaw in his flying. We got up about 3,000 feet and he told me on the intercom, "Did anyone ever tell you how you can lose power on this thing, and by manipulating the prop, you can slow down its fall like a parachute?":

"Hell no," I said, "And if you try it, I'll shoot you right between the ears."

He cut the engine off and we fell like a rock for about 800 feet. I left everything at the 3,000-foot level. Sure enough, he did something to arrest the fall. The sweetest music this side of heaven was when he engaged the clutch, or something, and started that beautiful engine again. But this guy could, and did fly the thing upside down and every other way.

The guys who flew the L-5 and the L-19 were worse. They were crazy but expert. If they had not been so expert, they could not have been so crazy. The L-19 was bigger and more dependable, so they said. But these pilots didn't worry about either. A few of them were dispatched all over the South to work with ATF.

Hunter, a fearless World War II fighter pilot, was wild but one of the best fliers in the world. He loved working with ATF. I think one of the reasons was that, although his antics would horrify anyone, maybe including our boys, the observers would say nothing. Maybe the seat upholstery in the observer's position became ragged after a few days, but Hunter knew they had guts.

I have known of this sonofagun finding a distillery in operation in the woods and dive bombing the operators until, in terror, they would run into an open field where he would buzz them so close they had to lie on the ground while other ATF agents picked them up. He would laugh like a maniac all the time.

Hunter loved to tease the agents. He would complain of having to piss, and land on a dirt road or, in one case, in a miniature, muddy little garden plot with weeds six feet high. This latter landing was merely a smackdown in the mud. Everyone told him the plane would have to be dismantled and hauled out on a truck.

"Naw," he said. "we can get it up without much trouble."

The little field would have been extremely short for dry and perfect conditions. At the end of it stood two large pine trees about five feet apart.

"Get the jeep and run it back and forth across the tiny field until the plane will roll over the mud. Now," he instructed, "pull it back on the south side just as far as it will go and we'll make a few practice runs." We followed instruction and backed it up with the tail sticking back into the woods at one end.

"Now," Hunter said. "Hold the sonofabitch back and we'll

catapult it by revving it up." This we did and he made a few practice runs.

He didn't even mention, or appear to notice, the impossibility of the two tall pine trees blocking the far end. When asked by the observer about how in hell he expected to clear the trees, he said, "I'll worry about that when I get there. You just walk out to the road and I'll land out there and pick you up in a few minutes."

After three practice runs he said, "Now boys, hold her back just as long as you can and we'll shoot her like a slingshot!" We did and then he gave us the far end. Everyone was afraid to look, expecting to see and hear a crash, explosion and fire.

But when the wild bastard got to the trees, he was already a few feet off the ground, and merely turned his plane into a complete sideways position and slipped through the trees just like he was used to doing it. I think he was. In a few minutes he picked up the observer and they were off to seek new thrills. All of this for a bladder break!

•••••

I worked with the choppers more. One complete day, a chief petty officer and I flew all over northeastern North Carolina searching for distilleries. We carried dynamite on the craft with us and when we spotted a moonshine outfit, we simply landed and blew the darn thing to smithereens. The caps (detonators) were carried by ground crews, who would meet us, provided they could find us.

On one occasion we found a distillery in the edge of some woods near a large cornfield. We landed in the cornfield. I got out and watched the de-acceleration of the prop. When the four blades lost momentum, one of the blades fell down on the ground beside the ship. I almost had a heart attack.

"Oh, don't worry about it," said the chief. "I've got a large nail in the toolbox."

A nail! Panic shook me. This nut had to be kidding.

He munched away on an apple and when finished, he fumbled around through a little box and found a large nail. It took both of us to lift the blade back into position. Apparently it had just lost a cotter pin and was unhinged. We put the large pin back through the holes and stuck the nail in the end to serve as a cotter pin.

After blowing up the still, we took off for the next one. And all four blades kept beating properly.

60

CHAPTER 5
THE TRACKLESS TRIO

You learn to tell instinctively, by the way the telephone rings when a momentous call comes. I knew this 9 p.m. call to our little rented house had to be a dilly.

"There's a helluva big outfit down thar in below Shiloh Church," said an excited tobacco road voice I recognized as Greg Myers. "I know hits there cause my 'nection done told me hit wuz. You boys oughta pay me big for dis'un for hit's a whopper!"

Dark clouds began to form in the back of my mind. Greg was a two-bit informer who pictured himself as glamorous secret agent X-9. He had seen too many who-dun-its and drag-'em-ins on the screen. No more than ten percent of his information had ever proven worth a damn.

But I had to go.

I endured the usual fuss-nag encounter with Jeri. Already I had put in fifteen hours this day. Another twenty-four more hours could easily go by before I got back home. Without any sleep, too. I slipped on my boots and called my crew. We would investigate, even though I had no confidence in Greg's generalities.

I picked up Chris and Johnnie. We drove the twenty miles to the general area. Greg's information was just that, a damn general area. We were shooting in the dark.

We parked the government car in a wooded place and started walking through the soft sand. After about an hour, we found an old road with fresh tracks impressed deeply. I instructed the boys to walk in the ruts made by the vehicles. We passed a house sitting almost in the road, continued to walk in the ruts for about two hundred yards. At a turnaround there, the main part of the traffic had stopped. But we later found that it didn't really stop, but cleverly dispersed and scattered, after which it all went generally north. This we failed to notice in the dark. "Goddamn sand is hard to walk in," Johnnie said. "I apologize, but the goddamn sand is still hard to walk in."

We scouted the ridges and the whole area. The terrain was slightly rolling, unusual for this coastal location. Scrub pine and white sand covered everything.

We criss-crossed all over the place. After an hour, we saw vehicle tracks where there should have been none. These tracks were a continuation of vehicular movement from the rutted road we had walked on and was then found disguised by scattering. Then we found more sets of such tracks several yards away. All seemed to be going in a northerly direction. We followed the tracks by flashlight to the top of a ridge where we doused the lights and continued by starlight.

About two hundred yards down the slope we found the several sets of vehicle tracks re-uniting and forming one road into a thick cluster of undergrowth.

"Damn!" I do believe we're going to find something!" Johnnie said excitedly. "Sure looks good!"

"But keep your voices down and your lights out. You never know what we're gonna run into," I cautioned.

These guys were the greatest rookies in the world but they still had to be guided closely due to their eagerness and their inexperience.

Silently, we examined a large clearing in the thicket. It looked like a great hall or room of some type. Inside the space loomed one hell of a big distillery! It was big enough to overwhelm us. New enthusiasm flowed into our tired bodies. We made a quick examination using lights after determining no one was present.

There is a uniqueness to a distillery. A trained investigator, familiar with the violators in his area, can usually identify the owner by the style and type of distillery. Written all over this one was the handiwork of Bully Brock, the largest violator in our seven county area. It had to be his. By pen light I went over it closely.

I attempted to ease back the cover off a mash vat. I felt a sting on my left wrist, like two burning needles. Out went the pen light and on came my large flashlight. There were two small scratches just back of my left hand. I swept the light onto the top of the vat and saw a large snake slithering off the edge and onto the ground. Security prevented the use of my .38. There was nothing immediately at hand to kill him with. The snake wiggled to the ground and disappeared in the thicket.

Chris and Johnnie were horrified. Immediately they forgot the monster distillery and started talking about getting me to a hospital.

"It's four miles back to the car and thirty miles to a hospital," I told them. "If it's a cottonmouth or copperhead, I'm dead anyway. Probably it's just a water type snake."

Some of the common water snakes resembled the poisonous cottonmouth and copperhead, and in the dark it had been impossible to tell which this was.

"We've got an all night job erasing the tracks that we have made all over this place, so let's get on with it," I suggested. "If it's a bad snake, I'll know within a few minutes and then we can attempt to get me out of here. Right now, I'm more interested in rubbing out these damn tracks we made so carelessly."

I tied my T-shirt around the artery in my upper arm. With a pocketknife I made two slices on the wound. The blood flowed freely.

It was vital that we eliminate all the tracks. Any good bootlegger unfailingly looked for any sign, especially tracks, that could have been left by officers. Bully Brock was extra persnickety this way. I knew he had the area combed over religiously each time someone came in to work.

With pine limbs and tops broken from the many scrub pines nearby, we began. I watched the snake bite wound very closely. Fifteen minutes went by and a little swelling started. This made me happy because I knew if the snake had been one of the lethal kind, my hand and arm would now be very much swollen.

So I forgot about the snake bite. It never did swell any more than it would have after a minor insect bite.

Erasing all our tracks took all night. We felt that we had accomplished our mission with the exception of the tracks that we had made walking down the access road. We had a brief brain stormer session.

"Have either of you boys got any rubbers (condoms) in the car?" I asked.

"Yeah, I got some in my knapsack," Johnnie said.

"Get the rubbers," I told Johnnie, "since I'm fresh out." Chris would never have had any because of his strong feeling about extracurricular sexual activities. Due to my eternal fight with Jeri, mostly about ATF, the only thing I had against it was the possibility of catching the clapp.

"Well, it's a long way back to the car," Johnnie lamented.

"Tell me where your knapsack is and I'll make the trip," I said. "I want someone to watch this operation until we catch Bully Boy."

I made the long trip back to the car in a run. I drove it down the road, using its trip in and out to erase the tracks in the ruts. At the turnaround I spit in one of the rubbers and threw it out. I hid the car and contacted Johnnie and Chris and learned nothing had happened.

It was now about eight a.m. I moved the car to another hiding place. I knew the operators must soon come. Since the best time to expect the big wheel is when a distillery is brand new, I thought we had an outside chance that Bully Boy would come today. This distillery was still under construction, needing the service of a plumber, or someone with a knack for setting things up. I knew Bully Boy could do this.

I had scarcely gotten back to the scene and hidden when two cars came to the turnaround and parked. There were five men in all. They all got out of the cars and with a load of equipment each, they walked toward the distillery.

We let them have plenty of time to get to the distillery, three hundred yards away, where they settled down to work. I stationed Johnnie at the turnaround after we removed the distributor rotors from the cars to prevent escape should they become alerted and panic. Chris and I advanced to a location where we could see part of the goings on. Throughout the morning we watched them work, trying to see enough of their features to identify them later. Bully Brock was not among them but I knew he might show up anytime.

About eleven a. m. I saw one of the men leave the distillery and walk to the cars. We stalked him. For him to try to start the cars might blow the whole deal, and we didn't want this. We followed him and he got into one of the cars.

He tried the starter and nothing happened. We were forced to take him and we did—quickly and silently. I judged him to be a lieutenant, not being dressed in rough clothes worn by still hands. He acted hostile and wouldn't say a word.

I ignored the part of the Rules of Criminal Procedures, whereby an officer is required to take a defendant forthwith before the nearest available United States Commissioner. Instead, we quickly took him over a hill, sufficiently distant from the others so they couldn't hear any loud vocal warnings or screams that might arise during his interrogation.

We handcuffed him to a tree. "We know that this is Bully Brock's outfit. Now you bastard, you're going to tell us when he will come here." For a long time he cursed us and didn't tell anything of value.

Several hours in the glaringly hot sunlight, without water, and exposure to some other techniques we used made him begin to falter. Then I hit him with the big cop syndrome. I told him he could get on our side, make as much money and have a hell of a better time. Leaving him in the hot sun with the silent Chris on guard, I went back in the direction of the massive distillery. After being sure the other distillery personnel didn't miss him, or either expect him back yet, I returned.

The lieutenant was ready. "Okay, dammit, what will I get out of this?"

"The best deal in the world. I'll see that you aren't tried, put you on government subsistence and let you work for me, and I'll personally speak to the judge."

"I'm ready. Bully will be here to bring a portable water pump, some yeast and some other stuff about 1: 30. He'll be driving a red and white International pickup. He will go to the still, see that the pump is set up right, then he will leave."

It was then one p.m. Leaving Johnnie this time to entertain our guest, we decided to watch for Bully at the turnaround. A shouted warning could be heard by Bully at the turnaround, but I knew Johnnie would get up on the prisoner's head if he so much as opened his mouth.

Precisely at 1:30 p.m., we heard the sound of a pickup coming down the access road. I had chosen this location because we would be within four feet of Bully as he paused, and thus could identify him. He passed right between Chris and me. We could now both identify him. In the back of the truck, we saw a portable gasoline motor with a water pump attached. The sound of the truck stopped at the distillery and then sounds continued.

In about thirty minutes, Bully came out right toward our position. He minutely examined the ground for signs. He acted suspicious. He walked to the turnaround and looked at the vehicular tracks I had made. Then he saw the rubber and the napkins I had thrown out. A big smile came over him. He appeared to be perfectly satisfied with his interpretation of the evidence. Obviously, he thought the intruders there had been lovers.

Slowly he started back toward the distillery. Now! It had to be now. I knew a wild raid might result in his escaping. But here he was in the bag. Our evidence on him was sufficient.

Bully didn't earn his nickname by playing softball at church. I hoped some of his toughness remained because I was getting bored and craved action.

I grabbed him from behind, placing a hand over his mouth to prevent an alarm. He struggled fiercely. Though fat and flabby, he fought like a tiger. I had to fight the bastard with one hand, refusing to let go of the grip on his throat to keep him from screaming warnings to the four men who remained at the distillery. Finally, I succeeded in overpowering him, and hustled him to another tree beyond hollering distance. I handcuffed him to the tree. Taking him to the commissioner that minute never entered my mind.

Four men continued to work at the distillery, a large, young, redheaded fellow and three black men.

My manpower was all used up. Both Chris and Johnnie had to guard the two we had already caught. That left me to raid the distillery and try to catch as many as I could of the other four men. Was I going to try to catch four panicky men?

I told Johnnie and Chris I would grab all of them that I could and try to run the others in their direction.

Slowly I went back to the top of the ridge. About one hundred yards from the distillery sat the big redhead, eating a snack. Wonderful! Maybe I could bypass him, go to the others and have Redhead between Johnnie, Chris and me. I circled Redhead without alarm and then entered a dense thicket. The three blacks were hard at work. I walked up and grabbed two, letting out a loud yell. The third untouched black quickly disappeared into the thicket. The other two fought like leopards.

A hard, short left hook behind the right ear flattened one man. Fortunately, he stayed down, apparently unconscious. The other bit, kicked, elbowed and tried desperately to get away. Finally, I chopped him with the edge of my hand directly in the throat. He went down incapacitated. Speedily, I put the cuffs on the first man who was coming around. Then I ran back up the hill toward Redhead.

He had heard the noise and was puzzled. I ran toward him and gained about eighty yards due to his confusion. Then he ran right toward Johnnie and Chris and the prisoners! I chased him until I knew they could hear me.

"Chris! Catch the big redheaded sonofabitch. He's coming your way!"

Chris left his position and made it part way back down the hill where he blocked and apprehended Redhead. Although Redhead was the youngest, strongest and should have been the toughest, he gave up like a lamb.

I went back and talked to Bully Boy. He was highly pissed off.

"How goddamn long do you think you can keep me here? You know that I know my rights. Everything I been hearin' about you must be so."

"What have you been hearing about me, Bully Boy?" I asked.

"I heard that you were the worst sonofabitch this territory has ever had. That's what I heard."

"Tell the people who told you that, that I appreciate the compliment," I said. "It makes me proud for a no-good bastard like you to think that about me."

"What about the commissioner?" he shouted.

"Coming up, just as soon as we can dynamite your rig down there and get you to town. Should be there by, say eleven o'clock tonight. How's that sound?"

He groaned.

My personal attitude, and you could get away with it in those days, was to hell with the commissioner. But I was about out of blank, signed search warrants. I could get some more since we were bringing in five defendants. The commissioner worked on a fee basis. Only after he processed his quota for the quarter did he become a sonofabitch to deal with. Until then, we were always putting more butter on his bread, thicker than he had ever experienced.

We made the mistake of dynamiting a fifty-five gallon drum of gasoline at the still and catching the whole area on fire. The blast depleted the oxygen in a sizeable area each time and without oxygen the fire couldn't survive. We also fought the fire with several water pumps salvaged from the still.

Coming out of that location in three vehicles, we went out of our way to make all the tracks we wanted.

We had not slept in almost two days, but catching the moonshining daddy rabbit and his henchmen kept us laughing all the way home.

67

CHAPTER 6
BACK TO LITTLE NATION

I was offered and could not refuse the group supervisor's job in Wilkes County, North Carolina, where I had broken into ATF. This was the number three job in the state in rank, pay and responsibility. I was to have twelve agents under me, including the aging Carlton Fine and other old friends I had worked with.

I reported and had a session of grab ass with my old buddies and made acquaintance with new ones added since I left. One was to become the best friend of my life, David Edwards, a graduate of Appalachian State University and a first class athlete, pro football size. He was aggressive, brilliant and witty. On top of that he had the sweetest wife in nine states. She was a registered nurse who looked after Dave as if he would break like glass. Jeri didn't like her at all. I told Dave it was too bad his wife couldn't have been twins so I could have had one of them.

I succeeded Jonathan who was promoted and transferred nearby as special investigator. Jonathan and Dave also were good friends as were their wives, who had been schoolmates. In Jonathan's zeal, he had not been content to nail the local criminals for bootlegging, but took it upon himself to raid poker games and report any petty alleged moral violations. In the process he made enemies of almost everyone in town. He had very thick skin and cared not at all how much abuse the people heaped on him vocally.

When I came on the scene it was not possible for a federal agent to cross the street, ride by in an automobile, walk across a field, go shopping with his family or appear anywhere without being abused, usually being called a sonofabitch. All the boys complained bitterly about it. It was a genuine problem. Informants were reluctant to assist us since they thought we were weak to put up with this crap.

My first official act was to have a post-of-duty meeting with this problem as the main topic.

I told the men that I was aware of it, and regardless of the

69

policy of my predecessor, that we would not tolerate it.

"How are you going to stop it?" someone asked.

"If you have to ask that, we have more of a problem than I thought," I replied. We agreed that it would stop. The only restriction that I put on them was that they should be careful with firearms.

Shortly thereafter I was stopped at a traffic light when a truck, known or suspected of hauling raw materials for moonshining, passed. The driver stuck his head out and rattled off something I didn't hear plainly, but it sounded like sonofabitch. The lone passenger smiled broadly. I followed the truck out of town and put my siren on him. Both occupants jumped out and met me at the rear of the truck. We were all standing face to face, eyeball to eyeball.

"Did you say something back there?" I asked.

"I don't know, by God, if I did or not," the driver answered.

"You're an absent minded bastard aren't you?" I asked.

He moved toward me and his partner took a step toward me too. "Well, there's no need standing here and arguing about something you won't admit and that I can't prove," I continued. "So I'll put it this way. If you gentlemen did not curse me back there, I humbly apologize for stopping you and taking up your time. **But,** if you called me a sonofabitch, like I think you did, you would crawl over a hundred whores to frig your dying mother."

If those aren't fighting words, they don't exist.

The passenger jumped around in front of the driver and I repeated my challenge. Since he acted so aggressively, I told him it particularly applied to him.

The two men leaned back and forth as if they wanted to fight and then as if they didn't want to. If a man turns several colors, they turned all of them, but neither made another move. Finally, they turned and walked back to the cab. I left them and returned to my office.

The next day, I had another meeting and passed this technique to the other men. Dave was elated! This was right down his alley and it was highly unlikely anyone would challenge him. He was a real hoss.

Several more incidents, in which this little tactic was used by different agents , completely stopped this public lack of respect.

"Bull" Blanton, a 320-pound member of our staff, had to hit one man because of it. With a back stroke of his open hand, he broke the neck of the suspect. Luckily, the guy was under arrest for a violation when he started his verbal abuse. Bull didn't know his own strength.

Nick got several reports about our campaign against this disgraceful abuse and told us to taper off and grow more thick skin.

"Bull shit, Nick," I told him. "I've heard how you kept the bastards under control in past years, and I don't think you really mean what you say." He managed a crooked grin that gave him away. He was delighted.

As a result of this campaign I got several calls late at night by violators, threatening to burn my home, harm my kids, and other violence. Through experience I knew that the man who tells you this crap wouldn't do anything. My answer always was, "What makes you think you have a monopoly on burning houses? I can burn your house, shoot your kids, or blow up your automobile just as easily as you can mine." This rebuttal proved effective.

The word got around that I was meaner than the bootleggers. Not so, just a bold use of psychology. At any rate, in short order we changed the public image of ATF one hundred percent.

After the short period that it took our twelve agents at Wilkesboro to reestablish a proper degree of respect for the "likker dicks," we settled down to break the backs of the violators in Northwestern North Carolina.

Several of my men reportedly had not worked in other areas and had been "Siberia-ized" to our post, which was rated the most active and most difficult post in the entire country. In the typical case, the unwilling transferee had been declared guilty of a bad attitude, a coverall term used by some half assed supervisor who really constituted the real problem himself. If he is right in his judgment that the man should be transferred, the supervisor seldom had the guts to tell it like it was. He wanted to nail the agent with the detestable term "he has a bad attitude."

I found these men, in a great majority of cases, to be just as eager, dedicated and often more determined to do a good job. To me they were no problem except most of them initially had the idea they had gotten the shaft. But after a few months, all would have cried if they had been transferred out of our environment in Wilkes County.

Another misconception, Wilkes was branded as the Moonshine Capital of the World. Some residents were proud of the title. Some even displayed on their little license plate slogans saying, "Wilkes County, Moonshine Capital of the World."

While major illegal liquor activities ran rife here, it was not the fault of a great number of people. Their integrity and honesty to me appeared to be well above the average. Later in my career I became disgusted and disillusioned due to the apathy of the courts and the juries and the public in other areas about the enforcement of the federal liquor laws. But not so in this county! In Wilkes, if a man was indicted on a strong case and went to court, his neighbors, associates and acquaintances would hang his ass.

In challenging this dubious title, I can say that the first distillery I found in the eastern part of North Carolina was at least twice as large as anything that I have ever seen in the northwestern part of the state.

We had a request from the sheriff of a far western county for assistance in doing an undercover investigation. Having been gone for a while and gambling that I would not be recognized, I decided to tackle the job myself. I joined Jonathan, who had received the request and was at that time stationed nearby.

The problem was the sale of "red" or bonded whiskey in a dry county to college kids by a couple of clubs and two taxi firms. I got a motel room and spent several hours fabricating a story that would be accepted. I decided to hit the joints and the cab companies with the story that I was a teacher here for summer courses. My story worked like a charm. But a careless error caused me trouble, though I succeeded in the overall operation, to pull the most colossal boner of my career. The only reason that I succeeded after this mistake was because this particular violator I was dealing with at the time was just a little more stupid than I was.

I was using my personal car at the time, and unknowingly, had let an envelope with my name, title and address from the U. S. Treasury Department, blow off on the floor between the end of the right front seat and the door.

In short order I had made undercover purchases from several joints and from one or two taxi drivers. I visited another taxi company and saw the "Wheel" standing in the parking lot. I pulled up to him and told him that I was a teacher here for a summer course and asked him where the ABC store was.

"Man, we ain't got no goddamn ABC store in this town," he said.

"Well, where in hell can I buy some booze. I'm supposed to get with some friends in a little while and I need four pints."

He questioned me closely and seemed satisfied. "Go around the block for ten minutes and come back to the parking lot right here," he said.

I did this and came back. He was standing there with a large bulge under his jacket. I pulled up and he opened the right front door. The damn envelope fell out on the ground and he picked it up.

He started to hand it to me, then read aloud the title..."Criminal Investigator..."

I took it from his hand and said, "Let me have my mail."

"What kind of goddamn investigator are you?" he snarled.

"I just told you that I am an insurance investigator," I insisted. Quick thinking, I thought, but knowing I had just told him I was a school teacher a few minutes go, I assumed the jig was up. I expected gun play any second.

The stupid ass said, "Oh, okay," and sold me the booze.

This was unreal. I couldn't believe it. I had almost killed myself with a careless mistake. It dampened my ego and made me wonder if I was at least a little retarded.

CHAPTER 7
THE CLIFF HANGERS

"Thar I wuz high up near th' top uv ole Whitehead Mount'n, mebbe not more'n a mile frum th' Parkway, when I seed this black plastic pipe a-snakin' up th' mount'n side. Skeered me. I think I knowed whut hit means. An' I think you all knows whut hit means. I kinda wanted to foller it. But I holds muh hosses. I knows better. I knows them high mount'n moonshiners gits mighty mean wid snoopers. So I figgers th' next best thing is come tell you boys 'bout hit. 'Bout that pipe, I mean."

"You did exactly right, Creighton, just exactly right," praised Stan Caple, slipping two folded bills into the jacket pocket of this sturdy oldster who scoured the Watauga County mountains searching for wild ginseng, a marketable herb used in medicines. The money equalled more than Creighton made in several days of herb hunting.

Stan, one of my best agents, and a native mountain man himself, was able to develop instinctive rapport and confidence with these mountain people. Creighton's tip was a prime example of how handsomely this rapport paid off. Elated, he hurried to me with the big news.

"This may be the one we been trying to find for a year," Stan bubbled. "Big Ed's probably. We've covered that part of the county but it never occurred to us to look high up near the top of Whitehead. That's damned rough terrain in there below the Parkway. Likely they have to pump water through a mile of plastic pipe. Access would be a problem. Probably from a road off the Parkway."

"Well, what the hell we waiting for?" I said. "Let's drive over and take a look around and make some plans."

This was Stan's territory so he called the shots. We stayed away from the Parkway roads and drove the valleys and opposite mountain sides, hoping to maneuver where we could glimpse the approximate location.

Fifteen miles from Whitehead, we abruptly met a large

truck, the driver of which we instantly recognized, and he us. Stan screeched to a stop, jerked the car around and sped back in pursuit over this narrow, extremely crooked mountain road. As we drew near again, the contraband was clearly visible on the back of the truck.

"Hell, look at that!" I half shouted. "Bags of sugar. Bags of meal. Bags of coke. Boy, we got us one here, Stan! Stay with him, boy!"

Although our government car was a Mickey Mouse conventional sedan with the damndest cheapest engine that the bidders could furnish, we still closed in on the loaded and laboring two ton truck.

The driver knew he couldn't outrun us. So he let his passenger step out of the cab while in full flight, something like eighty miles per hour, and he crawled up on the body of the truck where he began fiddling around with the bags.

Almost too late, I realized what he was doing and yelled a warning to Stan.

"Watch it, Stan! The idiot is bombing us with bags!"

Here came a one hundred pound bag of sugar splatting on the pavement and tumbling and partially disintegrating around the front of our car.

Miraculously, Stan kept dodging these bags dumped in our path, two or three a minute, for the next five minutes. A bizarre obstacle course for the best drivers.

Meantime, I had my .38 out the window shooting at the truck tires. I desperately wanted to shoot the bastard on the back of the truck who was trying to kill us. But I forced myself to keep my aim low. I succeeded in puncturing a rear tire on either side, but the remaining dual wheels carried it on since the gross weight now had been considerably lightened by that bag heaving bastard on the back.

The inevitable happened. No driver anywhere could have dodged the tumbling bags any longer than Stan did. The next one got us on the right front wheel, breaking it off from the axle. Our car spun off a curve and slid two hundred feet down the mountainside.

Neither of us was hurt, except our feelings of disgust and keen disappointment. We had lost the battle. It was one hell of a long walk back to a place where we could call for help. A bright little pedestal kept forming in my mind on which I etched the word "REVENGE.'

This happened just at the time when the ATF bookkeepers in Washington, D. C. had banned the use of firearms by ATF field personnel. But I didn't worry about it. I simply didn't report it. If someone had reported me, I would have simply "DENIED THE ALLEGATIONS AND DAMNED THE ALLEGATORS."

Stan decided we could only approach the suspected still location from the flatlands, climbing the mountain to make the investigation. He pointed out that we could go by vehicle to the Parkway, take a desolate dirt road and come down the mountain for a short distance, eliminating the torture of this almost perpendicular approach. However, to take this so-called easy way would almost certainly expose our presence.

We decided to make the initial search alone, determine when the rig would operate, if in fact we found one, then organize a raiding party and return in force.

Stan and I were both in excellent condition, working in these hills every day. But the seven mile climb to the top would be hell and we both knew it. Still we were very eager to do it, as it was an insult to our reputations to allow a huge distillery to go undiscovered more than a week or two. And this one could be a year old.

We planned to leave at dawn the next morning and travel light. We hoped to locate the distillery, reconnoiter it and learn all we needed to return with a raiding crew. If we were lucky, we could be back by nightfall. But only if both of us were in superb physical condition.

I went home and announced to Jeri my plans for leaving at four the next morning. She blew up. She was not worried for my safety. She would have been just as pissed off if I had planned an all night gospel singing. Her main worry was that I might awaken her in my early morning departure. She kept on and on. Finally, her hell-raising turned into one of those matrimonial filibusters. She decided to carry on all night.

After several hours and having undressed, I got so annoyed at her that I kicked, with a bare foot, a fiberglass suitcase sitting in the bedroom. The side crushed in and my foot went through the side. That is, all except for the little toe, which broke near the base and stuck out awkwardly like a broken toe.

She got a big laugh out of this, finding it very funny.

"Damn you! I should have hit you," I growled.

"Go ahead," she said, sticking out her pretty chin.

I didn't hit her but I had to ventilate my anger by hitting

something. I chose the closed bedroom door. The door was hollow and made of cheap material. The door jumped from its mountings and flew across the room, leaving a large splinter hanging on the hinges.

Then, the straight-out toe and its searing pain hastened me to the hospital to have it checked. I went to the emergency room at three a.m. and the nurse on duty examined my toe. "I believe it's broken. What in the world happened?" she asked.

"None of your damned business," I snarled. "Just rearrange it or call a doctor or something."

She put me on a waiting list and after a short time, a sleepy doctor came in. He had the toe x-rayed and confirmed it was broken. "Stay off it for several days," he said as he set it and splinted it up.

"Yeah!" I thought. Stay off it like hell. This day I would make one of the worst mountain climbs of my career. Damn the toe.

By now it was breakfast time. I had already filled my pack and brought it along with me, thinking I would not return home to awaken my lovely spouse. So after a country ham breakfast, I met Stan about an hour late.

"Where the hell have you been?" he asked. "I called your house and your wife hung up on me without telling me a damned thing."

She hasn't changed a bit, I thought.

I tried to ignore the throbbing pain in my little toe. Later in the day it was impossible to ignore it. A couple of shots of "evidence" from the evidence canteen helped. Having a second canteen, I filled it from the jug to help the pain, unbeknownst to Stan.

We drove twenty miles to the flatlands in another county and hid the government car. The peak in question was visible and looked fierce for a trip on foot. And fierce it was. It was hell to keep up with the forty-one year old Stan, especially with the toe. Only a frequent sip from that second canteen kept me going.

On and on we climbed up what appeared to be worse than a 180-degree incline. Toward noon the terrain improved and the woods thinned out. It became more the top of the mountain rather than the almost vertical side.

A little after noon we crossed the telltale plastic pipe reported by Creighton. Following the pipe for about half a mile, we found the monster still. It was situated on a shelf carved out of the side of the mountain. Access roads had been constructed, no doubt with heavy bulldozers, from the direction of the National Parkway. The neighbors likely were paid to report any officers or strangers seen in the area and to forget the bulldozing.

The outfit was not in operation so we had an easy time examining the mash and the layout to formulate a raiding plan.

From the appearance of the distillery it had been here for a year. Certain modus-operandi convinced us that it belonged to Big Ed, one of the area's largest moonshiners, a top dog in liquor production and physical stature. He was in most cases an untouchable. He had hirelings to operate his distilleries and market the product. But when one is operated this long, even the biggest of operators will sometimes become complacent and participate physically. We hoped Big Ed would do this.

We estimated it would be ready for operation in two days. The trip back down the mountain was not too bad, as I had refilled my second canteen at the still for medicinal purposes. However, by the time I got back to the city, the foot was almost twice its normal size and I was about drunk.

Stan was ecstatic. Big Ed was an old adversary whom Stan had been trying to catch for years. This time we had a chance and were gambling that Ed would put in an appearance due to the fact that this outfit had been in place so long he probably thought he had a license.

Jeri showed no sympathy for the terrible toe situation. She said she should have married a better husband. I agreed and invited her to do so.

"I can't, I'm religiously opposed to second marriages," she said.

"Hell, I'm religiously opposed to first marriages. I think a second one should be felony," I told her.

Early the next morning, we selected the crew to take back up the mountain the following day. I had a new man. That is, new to the distillery investigating business. His name was Darrel Pepper, and we called him "Hawk." He had been with the service about a year, but had been assigned to undercover operations all that time. He was from Tennessee and had started his career almost from the first day in undercover work. His success had been phenomenal, mainly because he looked so much like a bootlegger and talked so much like one that he could purchase whiskey from anyone, and often did. He had made so many cases against all sorts of violators that he had an ego problem. He thought he was just as good in any assignment.

Gus Talbert was our next selectee, being Stan's partner in working this territory. Stocky, short and as hairy as a bear, he hailed from Los Angeles. He was also a pork-eating Jew. A very good friend but so much out of place in this Southern moonshining environment that he couldn't stick his finger up his ass with both hands. However, he was very willing. On a raid he was so slow he couldn't catch the clapp in a whorehouse.

Our last selectee for the raid was Smitty, also a big city boy, but one whose many years of training here had helped him develop a high degree of proficiency.

So it was the five of us, once the plan had been memorized, who began the tough journey.

"Goddamn," exclaimed Hawk, when we reached the flat-lands and viewed Whitehead. "You mean we got to climb that monster?"

"That's right, Hawk, not quite like undercover work is it?"

"Wal, if you old bastards can make it, I sure can."

Hawk was only twenty-five years old but had a full set of dentures, long stringy hair, slightly stooped shoulders and talked like a mountaineer, which he was. He put a chew of tobacco in his mouth, got it juiced up good, then took out his dentures, pulled the stringy hair around his face and stooped a little more. "No damned wonder that guy can buy whiskey from anybody," I said to myself. "If I was a bootlegger, I would think he was an old customer."

With the heavy packs, we set out in a drizzling rain and very cool weather. Stan's woodsmanship led us in the right direction, mostly straight up. This time we had much more weight to carry, including fifty pounds of dynamite, since we intended to stay until the operators, and hopefully Big Ed, made an appearance, even if it was a week.

The damned little toe by now was somewhat better, but it was still giving me hell. Knowing that I would need medical assistance, I had secretly visited the evidence jug again before leaving.

It became backbreaking to find a foothold, grab a tree and pull ourselves a step at a time under the large packs. Gus began to tire almost before we started, and he slowed us down throughout the day. Stan and I got along much better, but we had to wait on the others frequently.

It was huff and puff, rest, take a few more steps, rest again.

80

"Hell," I thought, "I'll have to give these guys physical training when we get back."

Because of these problems, it took us all day to reach the slope where the incline decreased. Another thirty minutes and Stan and I found the plastic pipe.

Taking a rest, we again went over the plan. I laid out a contingency diagram. Each man was assigned a position to circle once we reached sight of the rig, provided it was in operation. If it wasn't, we would encircle the area and wait.

Our crew looked like a school of mink saturated with sweat.

Leaving the crew to the rear for a rest, Stan and I went on the back side of the distillery. The first visible sign in the now semi-darkness was a mountain of empty sugar stacks, which had accumulated over the past year.

Crawling on our bellies, we circled the scene and determined that it was not in operation. Quickly we checked the prime mash, noting happily that it was exactly ready for distillation.

We returned to our bedraggled crew for a pow-wow. Gus was detailed to creep up to the backside of the distillery until he was in sight of the sugar bags, after which he was to work his way up the hill to the left for twenty-five yards. There he would wait until the operators appeared and either Stan or I flushed them out. Then, of course, he was to apprehend anyone running near his position.

Such was the assignment of Smitty. Stan wanted the honor of putting his lawful hands on Big Ed in the event that he made the mistake of coming to the scene. Hawk, being totally green in this phase of law enforcement, was to follow me and assist as he could.

Realizing that we could possibly be here for days, though not likely, each man departed to find his position. A fine drizzle sifted down. Our major exertion over, we grew colder and colder.

Hawk and I worked our way into the makeshift shed used for protecting sugar and other materials from the weather. We began to devise some protection from the rain. Hawk donated his poncho for covering and we strung it out between four small bushes. After this, for a short time, the rain could not get to us but our wet clothes made it so cold I thought we might not be able to move fast enough when the time came.

Rummaging in my pack, I found a rolled-up suede jacket, the only dry thing in the whole pack. I took off all my upper clothing and put on the jacket. Man, how good to be dry! It felt like a fur-lined dinner jacket must feel. Nothing had ever made me so comfortable. Hawk used an old field jacket for the same purpose.

Within an hour, I noticed the rain had filled the head section, or hood, of the one-piece poncho. Being eager to please the boss, Hawk whispered, "I'll fix it good." He poked a stick right through the middle of the bulging head piece. Like it had come from a pitcher of water poured by a bartender, the several gallons of collected ice cold rainwater spilled out the open face side right down into and under my previously dry jacket. I nearly collapsed. Then I nearly turned into an icicle. Now the damned jacket was as wet as everything else. I had no alternative except to cuss and consult my second canteen, now half empty. The evidence didn't warm me up much but it made me not care about being wet and miserable.

"This just ain't our day," I thought, saying nothing to Hawk about his booboo. I was hoping that the raid would work out in spite of these conditions. The thought of old Big Ed running this monster for a year made me forget most of the snafus.

We lay silently in the soft rain for several hours. Though the rain continued, there was enough moonlight to see a great fog over the area. The terrain at this point not too far from the mountain peak, had few trees, just a large one occasionally and some underbrush crowding in.

About three a.m. a set of headlights turned off the public road into the distillery road, visible for about half a mile. I woke Hawk, who began putting on his shoes. We watched the vehicle come closer and closer. It wound slowly down the rough road cut by the violators and pulled into the distillery premises. A black four door Buick backed up to the shed. Two men got out in the rain and one raised the trunk lid. The men were closer to the position of Stan. One of the men, I noted with a skip of a heartbeat, was big enough and fat enough to be Big Ed. I began crawling toward them with Hawk right behind me.

Suddenly, from nowhere, the fog lit up all over the area around us. The light disturbed and puzzled me momentarily. We could be seen easily by the violators at hand should they glance in our direction.

Quickly I looked back at Hawk. Then I knew! In getting ready to move, he had put his flashlight, lens up, in a rear pocket. Carelessly, he had moved the "ON" button when doing so and the damned flashlight illuminated the fog like a reflector.

I grabbed it with my hand and put the light out. "Hawk, goddamit, don't ever put the light in face up. Always put the business end of a flashlight in your pocket, pointing down," I hissed.

"I ain't worried about the fuggin' light," he whispered back. "A bigger problem right now is that I got my damned shoes on the wrong feet."

What else? I cussed under my breath.

Then our luck began changing. The violators, miraculously, did not look in our direction and did not see the light nor hear us.

We crawled to within ten yards of the Buick, and noticed the two men were unloading hundred pound bags of sugar. Before I could make a move, Stan tackled the big fat man and I heard him say, "This time, Big Ed, you've had it!"

Hooray! The big man first!

The young buck with Ed leaped off the shed and made two gigantic leaps toward freedom before I got my hands on him. The struggle was short but fierce. We did a good job of tearing up the muddy ground before Hawk and I subdued him.

Hawk did a good job assisting in the apprehension, at least enough to get out of the ass chewing I had been rehearsing for him about the flashlight and the shoes on the wrong feet.

We were elated. We had that old satisfaction about a good job well done under very adverse circumstances. We considered this adequate revenge for Big Ed having operated this damned distillery for such a long time. Too, this was one of the very few times he had been caught.

We sat in the Buick talking to our prisoners. Gus and Smitty were still in their positions. Then Stan called me to one side for a conference.

"Look, I've known Big Ed for a hell of a long time. He's always been cool, but right now he's as nervous as a whore in Sunday School. I believe he's expecting someone else in here too."

"Good, Stan," I said. "We'll wait. But I wouldn't be surprised if he isn't nervous because of the way you busted his big fat ass when you pulled him off that embankment."

"Nah," Stan said. "I've been watching him like an eagle. He keeps looking at his watch, and he keeps looking back up the still road. I tell you, somebody else is due here."

"Good," I told him. "we'll reorganize."

Stan was delegated to stay with the prisoners to guard them and keep them quiet. I went to the assigned position of Smitty, whom I found all right. and then to Gus's designated position.

"Gus," I called. No answer. "Gus, where the hell are you?" I said in a louder voice.

"I'm over here, chief," he answered.

Damned if he hadn't gone to the right instead of the left, leaving a large portion of the periphery open for escape by the violators, had the raid taken place in the usual fashion. I stumbled across the valley between where he was and where he should have been. I was annoyed at him. The bramble briars I waded through didn't soften my temper any. I found him huddled in a burned out mash vat, rolled out of the way.

"Gus, why the hell didn't you go to the left like I told you? This side is covered by Smitty."

"Ain't this the left, chief?" he asked meekly.

"Gus, pick up a damned rock and throw it, then try to remember if you are right or left handed."

He did so. "Well, creeps," he said, "I did go to the right, didn't I?"

I proceeded to give him what is known as a royal ass chewing. He humbly bowed his head and my heart took over. "Well, Gus, don't worry too much about it, but I'm going to make an investigator out of you if it kills me."

"I thought I was already the best one you had," he said in a husky voice.

With Gus, I rejoined the others. The homemade road to the distillery made a sharp, almost 45-degree turn just as it entered the distillery premises. The bulldozers had made a cut in the mountain there in making the road that provided a twelve foot embankment at the turn. This bank declined toward the distillery so that it was about level with the terrain at that point. It was perfect for running up the road and then up the bank.

With Stan guarding, Smitty, Hawk, Gus and I lay in wait in the distillery yard for any vehicle coming to the curve. At that point I would jump off the bank onto the vehicle. We could not wait for him to get to the distillery because instantly he would know that something had happened to Big Ed and his flunky. Then he would jam it in reverse and back out.

About 4:30 a.m., Stan's prediction came true. The lights of a large two ton truck came off the mountain public road onto the private distillery road and wound slowly toward us. Smitty and

Gus were to take up positions on the side of the road opposite the bank, and Hawk, now learning very fast, would make the jump with me off the bank onto the truck. We reached our positions quietly. The truck neared the sharp turn and the head lights told the driver something had gone wrong.

As he turned, I jumped wide and far, making it to the front body of the truck, which was loaded to the gills with all kinds of raw materials. Hawk didn't make it and landed on the ground beside the truck.

I reached over and grabbed the door handle on the right side and gave it a hard yank. It didn't move. The bastard had the doors locked and the windows up!

I hit the glass on that side with a flashlight trying to make a hole large enough to insert a hand and unlock the door, but I only succeeded in cracking it. Rolling over while the truck was still in motion, I tried the same tactics on the left door, with the same results.

That did it! To hell with the bookkeepers and their asinine regulations about not shooting firearms!

With my .38 I shot the left front tire, causing the truck to tilt hard to the left and be in danger of going over the mountain. Then I shot out the left front glass, being moderately careful not to hit the men inside.

There were three of them. The driver, petrified with fear, unlocked his door and jumped out. I tackled him and we tumbled down the mountainside. He struggled fiercely to escape, causing me to pound on his head a little.

Putting my light on him new elation surged. This man was Big Ed's number one lieutenant! "Damn!" I thought, "They're getting brave with this rig."

This number two man, Yank Porter, was a very desirable catch himself. He had the reputation for being treacherous with officers but he didn't show too much of it now. He was so scared that he excreted in his trousers, making the atmosphere quite unpleasant in his immediate neighborhood.

With him, I crawled back up the mountain to see who Gus and Smitty had caught. They let both the other men get away. The reason was that our plan called for me to take the passengers on the right side with Hawk, and for them to take the left side, specifically the driver. Since I had to improvise and take the driver, the others fled out the right side and vanished in the night.

Still, we were happy with the total raid. The number one

and number two men, plus one hireling. We celebrated by building a massive bonfire where we warmed up until daylight, and shot the bull with the prisoners. Big Ed had stopped looking at his watch and back up the road after the truck came.

That fire felt great and it made us hungry. We snitched rations left at the distillery by the operators and had a delicious breakfast of Vienna sausages, sardines and pork and beans, plus all the evidence we wanted.

The defendants had all been advised, at the proper time, of their constitutional rights. Shortly after daylight, we began the nearly all day ordeal of putting dynamite to the outfit. When, near the middle of the afternoon, all available evidence had been secured, and the last barrel boomed into the trees, we loaded up in the two seized vehicles and went home on wheels. Like medieval conquerors, we rode into ATF headquarters in style, sporting our victims.

After the hearings before the U.S. Commissioner, I went home to Jeri.

"Honey," I said humbly, "You're right. We don't spend enough time together, nor do we go enough places, just us. I've got a great idea! You see, there's this nice mountain that I have found. I think it would be great this weekend if we hired a babysitter and just you and me went up this mountain for a nice picnic. I know just how to find the top and I'm sure you will just love it."

She looked at my muddy, bloody, smelly face and clothes and shook her head. It didn't work.

CHAPTER 8
SHOOTOUT AT AFTER SIX

Wren Olson didn't seem to know that the slaves had been freed. At least, the many blacks in his employ thought he was oblivious of the emancipation. He had the market cornered on all logging operations in the county. He owned most of the pulpwood trucks, hired and bossed the drivers and laborers, and what he didn't own, operators owed him for the pitiful beat up mechanical nightmares of had-been trucks.

Most of the poor people had been born under his dominion and their fathers, brothers and cousins all worked for Mr. Olson. He paid them almost nothing and for such meager compensation, they got very little except abuse, cursing and sometimes even beatings.

We considered him a poor example of a human—a true, self-made sonofabitch.

While his logging business proved very profitable, he had another business just as good. In his neighborhood and throughout his county, the population was predominantly black. For the lack of a better industry and because they thought they could do no better, the blacks were ripe for continuous plucking.

On every human level, there must be some retreat from the routine, recreation from daily toil or endeavor. Wren Olson knew this very well. So he did something to further enhance his local riches. He opened a large old two-story dwelling into a "Club." A "Nigger" joint, to which the people could come on Friday and Saturday nights to spend what little they had left. Naturally Wren sold illegal booze there. Any kind of rot gut, stumphole liquor that would run downhill was good enough for his customers. He named the place "After Six" from a fancy club he once visited in a large city.

The local sheriff, as usual in such a place, was paid off. His salary with the county was only $300 a month. On this he had to feed four kids, a wife and buy votes each four years at the election. The county government got what it paid for—not much.

Wren got by very reasonably with the sheriff, only paying him $25 per week to allow him to operate. For this he had a liquor license, rented out the many rooms in the upstairs portion of the structure for a whorehouse, and even hired the prostitutes at times. In addition, the sheriff was to tip off Wren about the presence of federal agents when he could. This could not always be controlled since we didn't trust the sheriff, knowing him to be rotten, and we therefore avoided him. Wren knew, however, that the federals were restricted in enforcement on the retail level. They were instructed to concentrate on major manufacturers and to stay away from retail establishments generally.

The U.S. government is not too morally concerned with the sale of moonshine but rather the assurance that the steep federal taxes are paid on the stuff. So, even a joint such as After Six, though its volume was great for the area, did not constitute such a threat to the revenue of the United States. It was a perfect setup for Wren and a hell hole for young blacks hungry for a good time on weekends.

Wren never called the sheriff for assistance when trouble developed. He handled his own problems and they were few. He would kill a black who happened to get crazed enough on the mean stuff to pull a knife or start serious trouble. He would commit murder on the unruly blacks even when he was the only white man within miles. For all his evil, Wren was afraid of nothing. He would have challenged the devil if confronted.

The place became so notorious that the federal men were forced to begin considering a raid, mainly because informants assisting them on major manufacturers in other matters were being affected within their own families over the evil of the joint. And, too, some were unhappy because their own product was not being used there. They envied the outlet at the After Six Club.

It was for these reasons that a decision was made to raid Wren's place. Four federal men were assigned in the area. They were aware that Wren was a murderous and savage man, one who had killed many, and one whom they knew would kill again if he thought it served his purpose.

Stanley Knowles was the agent in charge at Verne, the county seat. He had several years experience and had a keen knowledge of his job. With permission from his superior, the raid was scheduled. Stanley knew that Saturday night would provide a better chance of success as the weekend volume of moonshine would be at its highest, thus giving them a better chance of seizure before it could be poured out. He also knew because of the large size of the house, the necessity of searching quickly. Wren would have to be watched by at least one man and he would have to have at least three more men participate in the raid. One of his regular men was away on annual leave.

On a Monday morning he called his branch office and asked for three men for the special occasion. His supervisor was reluctant, knowing that it was not the name of the game to raid retail joints. However, he was soon persuaded, probably because Stanley almost promised several new informants out of the results. The raid was set for the Saturday night of the same week.

Carl Story, a handsome man of twenty-eight, finished mowing his yard on that Saturday morning. He played with his two little girls, then had a peaceful lunch with his attractive wife, Phyllis. He had already told her that he would have to be away for the weekend on a special assignment. Being resigned to such occasions, Phyllis said nothing. She only silently wondered what hundreds of ATF wives had wondered thousands of times. "Why did he choose this?" But choose his career he did.

He packed a bag to join the force at Verne well over a hundred miles to the south. He oiled his .38 service revolver with care, put the bag into his government car, and picked up a fellow agent named Vance Hopkins. Together they drove sixty miles south where they picked up another agent, Jeremiah Wilhoit, continuing on to Verne.

Phillip Davidson was stationed at Verne as one of the four resident agents. Fate programmed him to participate in this raid. He had been scheduled to leave two days before for an extended undercover investigation. He had come down with an infected throat which now felt better, so he was to participate.

Preliminary planning for the raid had been completed Friday and the group was scheduled to meet at the ATF office this day at 4 p.m. Carl and Phillip were deeply devoted to their families. Both were doomed men. To them this was just another raid. So they had no way of knowing that these little family activities were the last of their lives.

The group met precisely on time. Along with Stanley Knowles, the leader, there were Carl Story, Vance Hopkins, Phillip Davidson, Bruce Culp and Jim Whitney. Six men. The plan was well organized on paper and called for a specific job for each man. Stanley, along with Carl, would confront Wren with the search warrant that had already been drawn up. That is, after entry was gained as a group, Carl would be assigned to stay with Wren and watch him closely. Wren was unpredictable only as to what kind of and in what amount he would exhibit violence. There was no doubt that he would do something of a violent nature.

Stanley would then block the front door and search each man who approached.

Vance Hopkins would assist Phillip, Bruce and Jim in a room-by-room search of the entire building. Each would begin in searching one room at a time.

A "paper" rehearsal was conducted, and it appeared that each man knew exactly what to do. Stanley admonished each, though they already knew Wren, as to how extremely dangerous he was, and told them that they should take nothing for granted. Each agent was ready.

The crew left in one car and made an effort to avoid being sighted by the sheriff. This was only half-hearted as they knew the bastard was too dumb to really give them much trouble. Still, they also knew that in the unlikely event that he suspected their mission, a quick alert would go out to Wren.

They departed at 7 p.m. on a hot, muggy mid-summer day with the sun hanging high. A considerable detour was made, of about thirty miles, much more to kill time than to thwart the sheriff. By the time they reached the target area, some twenty miles in the boondocks, night had set in and it was time for business to be peaking at After Six.

The tough crew hit both back and front doors simultaneously.

Strong though they were, the hinges gave way to the agents. Wren attempted to block the front entrance and shouted a message to a couple of flunkies. Stanley confronted him but so far there were no grounds for arrest. Stanley quickly read the contents of the warrant and handed a copy to Wren who pretended to wipe his rear with it and threw it on the floor. He violently cursed the agents but tried no other violence.

The plan went smoothly into effect with the assigned agents beginning their duties.

Carl Story, the agent assigned to guard Wren to prevent him from harming any other agent, tried to do his job. As he could not yet arrest Wren, there was only so much he could do. He could not place handcuffs on him nor could he put his hands on Wren unless he acted violent.

90

The room in which Carl and Wren stood was a large lobby type with a crude homemade bar across one corner. They stood near the bar while the others were searching. Wren leaned against the bar. Carl Story's keen eyes were fixed on him. Like lightning, Wren leaped over the bar, immediately placing it between him and Carl Story. Quickly he ducked under the bar, then raised with a .38 automatic pistol in his hand.

Carl's leap over the bar was a quick reaction and a great effort, but halfway, in mid-air, a slug from the wicked .38 blew his heart in half. He was dead before he fell limp across the bar.

Wren fired another slug in Carl's head, then pivoted toward the doorway of the nearest room where he knew another agent was standing.

Hearing the shots, Phillip Davidson charged through the doorway with his service revolver in his hand. Wren fired three quick shots and Phillip fell. His only shot went wild into the ceiling as he crumpled to the floor, killed instantly.

The other agents swarmed into the room. Vance Hopkins got off the first shot at Wren. His slug tore into the middle guts of Wren and felled him. The slug was a dum-dum and literally blew Wren in half.

Ambulances were called. For Carl and Phillip it was too late. Wren was still alive and was rushed to the hospital where he had emergency surgery.

One of the agents was posted at his door as a guard. Wren had no chance from the beginning. The operation necessitated the removal of a major portion of his intestines. When he did revive for a short time, he appeared to be in mortal agony. He cried and screamed constantly. He was told that both agents were dead but he seemed unconcerned about anything but his own pain. He only lived four hours and died a terrible death, crying to the good Lord for help.

The widows and children of Carl and Phillip were taken care of financially by the government, but this could never make up for their terrible loss. A memorial plaque with large photos of them still hangs in the main office of the state headquarters.

Two more ATF agents gave it all for very little.

They were added to the casualty rolls of the service which has more fatalities and injuries than any other law enforcement agency in the world.

CHAPTER 9
THE RALEIGH OFFICE

Rumors indicated the creation of at least four "area supervisors" for ATF in North Carolina. We already had twenty-six posts with one supervisor at each, plus three in Charlotte. So we needed more supervisors like we needed a case of hives. My record made me a prime candidate. The job entailed overall supervision of several posts and all kinds of government responsibility, including the spreading and development of law enforcement prestige.

What ATF was really trying to do was mimic the FBI. There is no way to equal that organization in the eyes of the public, although we already had the hell beat out of them in investigative ability, freedom of operation, and in every way except for their fabulous lab, their image and public relations that we commonly referred to as propaganda.

Their system is to make a quickie investigation to determine if a case is a lead pipe cinch and can be solved successfully. If it is not, then they relinquish jurisdiction to another agency. In this way their solid gold reputation is protected. Many of their glamor cases are really made by local law enforcement agencies.

I personally know of a bank robbery case in which a lone North Carolina Highway Patrol trooper arrested three dumb bastards who stuck up a bank using a red Cadillac hearse to make a getaway. The trooper found them quickly and an FBI agent joined him. Next day, newspaper headlines said "Lone FBI Agent Captures Bank Robbers." The trooper did not even get honorable mention.

Don't get me wrong. The FBI has many brilliant agents. But they are so hamstrung they can't breathe without approval and guidance from the Justice Department hierarchy.

Eventually, a statewide conference was called to select the four area supervisors. I didn't think we needed them but since it paid more money, I was interested. It was the only time I ever was in an election of candidates in the government service by other employees. All the group leaders were asked to vote for four men.

I was not too concerned about the outcome. Although it did pay more money, in every case it would require a transfer. And the money was not great. If supervisory jobs in government meant very much money wise, I would have been digging like everybody else. But I considered the difference to be insignificant. For instance, what the hell was $1,000 more per year? If each promotion had meant $10,000 more per year, like some industries, I would have been a politicking sonofagun.

I received the most votes and was given one of the jobs. I was stationed in Raleigh. I had not been to Raleigh many times and I was sure that Jeri would raise hell and try to block my moving. This didn't bother me too much because I was used to it.

My area was twice as big as any other, taking in all the territory from Durham to the coast. Right away, I decided that in summer months there would be a drastic need for supervision on the coast. The job had lots of travel and would keep me away from home considerably, relieving me of the intensifying verbal combat with Jeri.

In this assignment I made a lot of friends and some enemies. Raleigh itself, for instance, had a monumental personnel problem. It was caused by a sonofabitch who was a former officer who had created a racket for himself. Half of the Raleigh staff believed him to be a saint and the other half considered him a crook.

This brilliant and persuasive man ran a racket. Boy, what a racket! It was an extortion and protection racket. He knew every law enforcement officer in two states and cultivated them all. He would furnish them valuable information only on those violators who would not pay him to protect them. Then he would extract more information from the officers' friends while they reported to him about other cases without the officers ever realizing they were giving him that information. Then he would sell this information obtained from the officers to his clients, that is, to those who were paying him high fees to protect them.

I conferred at length with all the personnel in Raleigh. The bitterness between the two factions was solid.

I ordered a telephone tap on his private line. I used two agents, one being proficient in electronics. We established a panel truck in the woods near his rural home and after finding his telephone "pair," we put on the tap.

94

At that precise time I had to go to Washington, D. C., for six weeks. I instructed these two agents that the telephone tap operation was illegal and warned them of the consequences. I told them that if they hit pay dirt to call me and no one else. I was not afraid of the consequences but I didn't want these two men getting fired or jailed.

Within three days we hit it big. The traitor called several big bootleggers, and related conversations that he had had with federal agents in which he learned the progress in major cases. He conspired with the violators about how he should get properly compensated without a flap. He complained that in many cases he saved several men from being caught and how he saved vehicles and equipment from being seized only to be screwed out of the fee.

The agent I left in charge of this operation got ambitious. He did not report this bonanza to me by telephone as I instructed. Instead, he reported through official channels.

Hell broke loose in ATF officialdom. Some panicked and everything was disrupted. They called a big meeting in Columbia and ordered the tapes delivered by the agents who obtained them.

I finally was informed by my agent of the facts after he had made his report. I told him that he would probably get fired and indicted but he said he considered the taped evidence too big to hold. I then called my superior and informed him that I had engineered the whole matter and that the other agents were simply taking orders. I asked to assume total responsibility for the wire tapping. My plan had been to take my damaging information obtained to the parties involved and let them hear for themselves. Then we could burn the tapes.

Herk in Atlanta got in the middle of it. Right away he started looking for a way to fire some people he didn't like, using this flap for an excuse. What a bastard!

The only action taken was a few transfers. Although everyone knew that I had done this thing, I was never talked to about it and never penalized.

It was absolutely devastating to the former officer. No one was allowed to speak to him again and his racket went down the drain. As far as I was concerned, it was a success. But some of the people who patronized this traitor were embarrassed and had quite a lot of bitterness toward me.

Happily, the whole thing resolved itself soon afterward when his wife caught him frigging around and blew his brains out.

•••••

My group leader in Raleigh, Grandy Boldt, turned out to be a great friend. He was a former state trooper and was my kind of down home folks. We shouldered through a lot of battlefields together, including a few shooting experiences, and we initiated some of the most unorthodox methods of obtaining information imaginable. Tactics we got away with were unbelievable. Like all good officers, Grandy had a certain wild and stubborn streak in him. He would take dangerous chances, most of which paid off with a good case.

My group leader at Dunn was just as good. But he soon left and I recommended Rick Hayle to replace him. Rick oozed low key brilliance and high octane action. Companionable and sincere, he was, without doubt, the funniest man in the world—and he worked his tail off, too.

Before I came to Raleigh, Rick was deliberately run down by a sonofabitch and literally wrapped around the drive shaft of a car. All the great nerves and fibers were torn from his spine. Unbelievably, after this, probably in shock, Rick ran the violator on foot for two hundred yards and arrested him. In this case, I felt that man should have been shot and a "dropper" left with him.

Rick worked for many years in pure torture. I had him transferred to Charlotte where the physical stress was much milder. He continued to work like hell. Then he got a medical retirement.

Rick, Grandy and I worked hard and played hard. In our off time we managed to get barred from most of the motels on the Eastern Seaboard. Somehow management just couldn't understand and wouldn't accept our antics and behavior.

There were many other sterling men in my area and I was beginning to enjoy this assignment. Normally it is the responsibility of the area supervisor to dress up like a Philadelphia lawyer, go to the office, and talk about motivation, incentive, etc., and develop rapport with the DA. I was already in with the DA and drank a lot of booze with him. The area supervisor was supposed to play executive and make only desk evaluations of his men. Not so with me! I put on my work clothes and went on every raid I could get in on.

This did not please the higher supervisors who never seemed to realize that we already had one supervisor per man, a ridiculous situation. Why the hell does a highly trained college graduate or a former local officer with years of experience, including making decisions in cases of life or death, need some Johnny-come-lately, usually a brownie point expert, to further supervise him? It got so bad we almost had to wear badges to keep from supervising each other.

Grandy proved a natural genius in obtaining information on huge distilleries, especially from black people. He could talk just like them. Many times I've heard him talking to the blacks. "Man, you got to tell the truth because de truth is the light and de light will set you free!" Casually picking lint from their clothes, he put his arm around them and the first thing you knew he had information on a 20,000-gallon outfit.

At Raleigh, we had several other good men. There was Mac Orville, a solid boy from Florida who never said much but who would back you up til hell froze over. Buck Tennessack came from Florida also, and he fitted into our system. His greatest attribute was that he was so well hung he started a legend. Buck was a bachelor and when the word got around, he was in great demand. He would get a little nervous when some girl called up complaining that he was late. We weaseled him out of a few little escapades.

Jesse Kildaire was a literary genius. The dictionary contained no word that he could not spell, define or pronounce, probably backwards. He later retired and reached some fame by writing a book. While he had a world of talent, we remember him best as the only man in the world who could stand flat footed and piss over a 1956 Chevrolet.

Henderson, forty miles north of Raleigh, was one of my posts. We had four good men there too. They were so damn good that they were not satisfied catching bootleggers sixteen hours a day. They began to quarrel with each other.

Twice I went there and conducted one of those Washington, D. C. management meetings in which I tried to resolve the problem by instilling in them the proper motivation. Neither worked and the infighting continued. Determined to win, I went back for a third try. I rented a motel room, bought two fifths of booze, and called the group leader and asked him to bring everyone to the room. We came up with a deck of cards and proceeded to have a non-Washington, D. C. management meeting. We played for a dollar a card until everyone settled into a hospitable atmosphere after a few drinks.

Judging the time to be right, I brought up the personnel problem. By that time, communication burst forth which was not forthcoming at the other two conferences. We discussed each man's feelings about the other and got all the bitterness out. We did have one little fist fight in the process, but it only served to further bring out the closed-in mis-apprehensions.

Our superiors never knew of this instant resolving of personnel problems. They would have roasted or fired us had they found out. I never had another single complaint about problems at Henderson. The men worked extremely well together afterward.

•••••

The Raleigh office shared the same one story building with IRS. The latter people were very apprehensive about us, having seen us come in to arraign prisoners in rough clothes, bloody and muddy from head to foot. We were a unique lot. They were, as a rule, highly trained, mild non-violent accountants. It is quite remarkable how they never reported us for some of our conduct after days in the woods, freezing and fighting the enemy. We had to bring in any prisoner immediately for appearance before the U. S. Commissioner and this process sometimes took several hours.

Some of those times being cold and abused we found it convenient to open up a bottle on government time. We worked very hard and we played hard. But our friends in IRS could not help but know about our playing. To my knowledge no one ever said a word about us.

BIG BAD CHASE

Rick told me about the big bastard in Dunn who had earned a rattlesnake reputation, having been suspected in earlier years of murdering his wife and baby girl and burning them for the insurance. No one ever proved that but he had a long criminal record of other violent crimes. He operated a little still in the swamps and he spread the word that he would kill any federal agent who got close to him. All the local officers avoided him like the plague since he towered six feet, five inches and weighed 265.

This big bad man drove a Ford pickup with a Cadillac engine. I was driving a 1960 Ram-Jet Dodge which was faster on wheels than anything I had ever seen. I asked Rick to let me know when he got some concrete evidence on the big bastard so I could help nail him.

One Saturday afternoon I got a call from Rick who said he had good information that Big Bad would load materials at his home that night to take to a distillery. We made plans to surprise him.

He lived at the end of a dead end dirt road about three hundred yards off Highway 301 at Dunn. I joined Rick that afternoon and was told that he would make his move about 1:00 a.m. Rick took a crew and set up surveillance around his house.

Customarily, Big Bad took his gun out to his front porch each night and fired a few random shots into the woods to scare off spies in the event he was being watched. Rick knew of this and was prepared. But no shots were fired this night.

Right about 1:00 a.m. I received a radio call from Rick who said Big Bad was loading propane gas tanks (used to fire a distillery) a small wooden boat, sugar and other commodities. Concealed behind a church nearby, I eased without lights to Highway 301 where I intended to block Big Bad when he came from his home. I sat there with the powerful Dodge engine idling.

Big Bad came right up to my bumper, driving without lights and didn't see me until I turned on my headlights. He made a hard right turn, evading my block, and tore up the adjacent lot reaching 301.

I chased him half a mile. The Dodge had absolutely no problem in overtaking the Ford-Cadillac. I turned on my light and siren and attempted to pull alongside Big Bad. He tried to knock me off the road and missed. We were probably making 120. I dropped back and decided to try another method.

I fell back and then pulled up again, trying to edge him off the road. This time he bumped the Dodge with the end of the wooden boat in his pickup. Again I backed off and decided to try still another method.

About one hundred feet behind him, I hit my siren. He misjudged my position, thinking I was just about on his bumper. I wheeled hard to the right, then hit the power, pulling up to his right rear. I put the accelerator on the floor and hit him with full force in the right rear corner.

That truck made two complete turn arounds in the road

99

and slid about 150 yards up the right ditch, jumping a new culvert, turned around again and hit a pile of sand on the opposite side.

The propane gas tanks tumbled about five hundred feet out into a field. The boat was splintered. The left front wheel sheared off and disappeared. We never found it.

Then the pickup bounced back across a hole onto 301 and he, believe it or not, drove it up the highway another two hundred yards without the left front wheel. He jumped out and ran.

We caught him on foot and the only mark on him was one little cut on his cheek. This was unreal, because I had seen his head lashing back and forth at the impact. It broke out the windshield, the rear glass and both side glasses. The truck could not be identified as to what make it was.

The wreck caused me to roll over in the road and overturn in a big ditch. My back felt like a dozen devils jabbed it with pitch forks. I had to go to the hospital emergency room.

Big Bad got five years for the caper.

Several years later, after serving his sentence, he put up a little still in an out building in his backyard. He didn't halfway try to conceal it. He lived alone now because his second wife moved out in mortal fear of him.

We went to watch the still one night when it was as cold as ten feet up a polar bear's rear. The next morning, after an uneventful night, Big Bad came out and snooped around. He found one of our agents and tried to cut his throat. He ran into the house with them right behind him.

He grabbed an M-1 military carbine off the wall and opened up. By the grace of God he didn't hit anyone.

One of my boys shot him through the center of the chest with a .357 magnum. He didn't even flinch, but kept firing the rifle for several seconds. We had to overpower him by hand with a few blows in the head with revolver butts. Within a few minutes, he was unconscious on the floor. The magnum slug knocked a hole just to the right of his spine as large as a half dollar.

We loaded him in his truck and rushed him to the emergency room of the Dunn hospital. He was given emergency treatment, then taken to Duke Hospital in Durham, North Carolina, where after about ten days, he recovered and was walking around in the streets.

Somehow he had made a $75,000 bond.

After Big Bad got out of the hospital, he arrogantly resumed his former activities, and we went back after him. I led the raid this time and placed two riflemen in front of his house, two at the rear, and I elected to sneak up to his bedroom window and put a tear-gas shell into the room.

It was three a.m. and not a light nor sound was evident. As I got to the window a flashlight beam hit me in the face. I dived into a ditch and noticed that he had walked out on the porch, probably to fire his random shots into the woods.

I felt sure that this time we would have to kill him. Somehow I rather savored this opportunity. After all, he had tried to kill me with the pickup truck years before, and he tried to kill several agents with the carbine.

By radio I informed the others that he had run back into the house. We were sure that he had gone after a gun. A moment later, he appeared on his lighted porch as naked as a jaybird with his hands reaching over his head.

We arrested him and took him back to jail. I asked him why he had taken off his clothes.

He said, "Listen, I'm not afraid of the troopers, the damn sheriff, nor the deputies, but ATF boys will kill your ass. I knew if I was naked that you couldn't shoot me."

Somehow, he made another $50,000 bond. He got out of jail, went home, poured five gallons of gasoline on his home and burned it.

For all this he got seven years in the pokey.

I predict that he will either kill some officer or be killed by one eventually

CHRISTIE

Christie was the playgirl for the ATF in Raleigh. She worked for IRS intelligence. A pathetically ugly person, she had crossed eyes and a very large upper torso. She didn't appeal to me at all. Christie was divorced, very handy and available, and she loved all ATF investigators since we were men who would go with her.

Many of our boys had a fling with Christie and she pursued me with a dedicated vengeance. By this time I had finally separated from Jeri, so Christie intensified her campaign to snare me. I escaped in every case. Hell, I had a new girlfriend who would make Marilyn Monroe look like Mickey Mantle. I didn't need Christie.

Top dedication to ATF work strains a field man's health and

stamina. I really believe that any ATF hard charger should be given full retirement after ten years because by that time he is burned out. One of the pitfalls is the constant involvement with, and use of, alcohol. There are a number of reasons: on bitterly cold days, alcohol warmed us. We drank when we were so exhausted we couldn't remain on our feet without some stimulant and there were more days to go. We didn't resist the normal inclination to use it in our periods of relaxation. So, it was after the use of alcohol that Christie became attractive to some. But she never became appealing to me, mainly because I felt sorry for her. I consumed my portion of the alcohol but Christie wasn't for me.

Christie's problem was extreme loneliness. I felt very sorry for her and was happy later when she met some joker from another state and remarried. Many times before that, though, I directed company to her.

One of my friends, when a little tipsy, would call her to his office when he had out-of-town visitors, usually other ATF personnel. He would reach into her dress and extract one of her enormous breasts and display it. Christie only giggled.

VISITATION SYNDROME

The government visitation syndrome prevailed as a necessary evil at any post. Big-time supervisors by necessity had to visit outposts for many reasons, audits, inspections, evaluations, etc. Naturally a post near a resort, like the beach, had greater need of visitation by those executives than the ordinary posts.

Visitors ranged from an area supervisor, which I was, to such luminaries as the chief of the national or regional office. In between these two men were a multitude of supervisors, totaling about one per mission man. This term means an individual occupied with performing the primary mission of the service, not occupied with seeing that someone else does.

Most supervisors I was under, an overwhelming majority, were superlative. My career favorite was Ray Hahn, a noble agent who went on to better things. Ray had been through the mill, accumulating his quota of shootouts and hard charging, tough cases. He would back up a subordinate until hell froze over and he didn't give a damn what anyone else thought as long as he thought it was right.

Most of the visiting VIP's would drink your liquor, eat your steaks, shoot the breeze, take your money in a poker game and even share the company of your girl friend if invited.

Once I was blessed by the visit of the number two, three, and four executives in the whole Southeastern United States. Their visit lasted two days. The wheels were accompanied by a small staff of assistants who were conducting a major evaluation of our area.

Number four executive turned out to be one of those that you don't fall in love with—ever. He came on strong and knowledgeable, but ran his mouth too damn much. One of our better agents was being tried in state court that day in another city for bastardy.

The wheel said, "Joe, since you're a bachelor now, you should go testify for old Bradford and tell the court you screwed the gal so he can get off the hook."

He was just joking, of course, but his comment stimulated a reaction in me, since I had trained the agent in question while stationed in the mountains. I said that I sympathized with the agent. But then I went too far. I made the mistake of commenting that Brad had always had a little stick trouble which interfered with weekend work while in the Blue Ridge Mountains, even to the extent that I had to talk with him about it.

Number four turned out to be one of Herk's listening posts. For reasons of his own, bucking for promotion or otherwise, he had to tell Herk everything and then some. He must have known that Herk was not particularly fond of me, since I refused to show any affection for a disgusting part of his anatomy.

Four went back to Atlanta and told Herk that I had said that if the government had fired Brad when he was in training, as I was alleged to have suggested, that the government would not now be in this embarrassing position, a complete and damaging lie.

I got a mean memorandum a few days later. The chief stated that I said so and so. I was ordered to make an explanation in writing about why I had made such statements. I made a simple reply and said, in writing, that number four had told a goddamn lie when he went back and reported to the chief. I got a letter of reprimand through channels from the commissioner, a copy of which went into my personnel file.

That was no problem, though. I was quite friendly with a cute little redhead who worked in the Atlanta office. She would gladly steal the copy out if I ever wanted it removed. However, I didn't give a damn whether it was in the file or not.

103

As usual, Herk used the situation to give hell to those who wouldn't provide him with his emotional need—that certain anatomical expression of affection commonly known as ass-kissing.

The next time I saw number four I asked him why he fabricated such a bunch of crap out of our previous conversation.

"Listen, we have been friends. We have drunk booze and played poker together, but I want you to know one thing, I am one hundred percent treasury agent, dedicated to my job in all situations, and one hundred percent loyal to my boss, whom I admire very much. My loyalty demands of my conscience that I report everything to him," he said.

I wondered where this intense loyalty and total dedication had gone the day the commissioner walked into number four's carpeted office and found him not giving dictation to his secretary. I didn't reflect these thoughts to him.

I had already dismissed the flap from my list of things to worry about. I was satisfied to get only the letter of admonition for being profane in official channels instead of getting fired for it. Even Herk, however, didn't want me fired. My job productivity and efficiency were huge assets to him.

I did cause Herk some frustration. He didn't want a man in a supervisory position, particularly one with executive potential, who wouldn't bow and scrape regularly. The next time I saw him in Atlanta he told me that he hated to always be putting me down when interviews came up for executive jobs. He admitted that in all interviews that I came out in the top three.

I told him I was aware of the fact that he didn't want me in an executive position and that while he was chief, I didn't want to work for him in that capacity anyway.

I said, "Herk, if all you want to hear all day is 'Yes, sir, you're right. Yes sir, that's exactly what I think,' then why in hell don't you buy one of those cheap Japanese tape recorders and say those things, play them back all day long, and fire me. It would keep you from having a lot of headaches and save the government a lot of money?"

He said, "You've always wanted to be on the racketeering squad, haven't you?"

"Yes sir," I replied.

"Well, if you will request that in writing, I'll give you my word that you can have it and stay in Raleigh as long as I live."

The special investigative section, or as we called it, the

racketeering squad, had been my sole ambition with ATF. Right then, Herk and I made a gentlemen's agreement and shook hands on it. I felt like Br'er Rabbit in the briar patch.

That one trip to Atlanta was the most productive of my career. Not only did I make a deal to reach my career ambition peak, I met the little redhead in the coffee room, enjoyed a chummy conversation with her, then rode on the elevator alone with her, to the seventh floor. We made some tentative plans for the next visit, tentative primarily because her husband was narrow-minded about her going out with good looking bachelors like me.

Too, I found out how tightly you can clinch with a beautiful redhead in an elevator for a few floors. That woman remains a genuine queen and trooper. Besides that, she had access to all the confidential files that affected the lives of agents in the field. And occasionally I needed some file searching.

CHAPTER 10
THE MASTER CRIMINAL

The Special Investigation Section's purpose was making cases on the major violators and super criminals, the big, big boys too tough for anyone else. We enjoyed more freedom of movement than any other agency in the federal government. Man, that was dreamy work for me!

At one time, the SIS had been used to turn people out to pasture and vegetate. A joke from earlier days said an SIS man carried a briefcase with nothing in it but a Playboy Magazine and a fifth of booze. In many cases this proved true. But I knew that a man could produce more for the government in this job than any other if he had the desire to accomplish something. Its challenge proved fascinating and irresistible for me. The only limit I saw was that big blue sky. It was like starting all over again at middle age.

My new chief came to Raleigh for a conference, briefing me on my new job. He said the section usually allowed a man to select his own cases but one top-priority criminal would be assigned to me as this one desperately needed to be caught.

My assignment to investigate the illegal liquor activities of Paul Barker, the master criminal, began as an exciting thrill and challenge. This was the biggest of the Big League, the ultimate goal in the ATF. The experience turned out to be tragic in almost every aspect—a spirit-shattering exercise in futility. Beyond all else, it was an education.

Paul Barker held charter membership in the original twenty men on the National Roster of Organized Crime. He had been featured in national magazines as King of the Moonshiners. For thirty years he had been in the big time liquor business and had made a liar out of the philosopher who said crime does not pay. He had accumulated millions and had served only one brief term in prison.

He and his brother had kidnapped a federal agent once, chained him to a tree, tortured him and left him for dead. For that he received a six month sentence.

107

A genius, Paul could have made empires in legitimate enterprises. But he had the same disease as most dedicated ATF investigators. Thrill and challenge pounded in his blood and he preferred the opposite side from law and order.

He owned dozens of farms manned by black tenants who thought they would starve to death without Paul. His greatest sin was the corrupting of little boys as soon as they got old enough to work at a moonshine still. Many never survived the life of crime he led them into.

Most of the magazines glamorized him as a type of Robin Hood. I called him a greedy sonofabitch who resented every dollar that he had to let go to charity by handouts or in any other way.

His personality and public relations would have complimented the chairman of the board of Ford Motor Company. He was a friend to such VIPs as the Governor of North Carolina (at one time), the Secretary of State of North Carolina, more than one state and federal judge, and most everyone else except aggressive law enforcement officers whom he hated with venom and passion.

I worked on him for several years. During that time he developed a new intense hatred for me.

Once he offered $100,000 for a hit contract on me. But he offered it to one of my good informers in Charlotte who was a big time official in the KKK. The man called me about it at 3:00 a.m. right after the offer was made. We were good friends and he had helped me in many successful cases.

In return I gave him certain assistance and technical advice about how to run his own liquor business and get by with it. I even made a few deliveries for him into cities that had an uptight police department. To me this was excellent reciprocal business, comparable to a good undercover investigation.

Anyway, I chewed him out for being so upset about the offer for my murder. I told him to go back to sleep.

"The next time you see Paul," I told him. "Tell him that maybe I will resign from the ATF and he can give me that $100,000 and then everyone will be happy."

Nothing could be further from the truth. Knowing I had him worried and edgy, I dug into him harder.

The first move was to develop a good network of informants. This proved extremely difficult for a number of reasons, mainly that everyone was deathly afraid of Paul because of his violent nature. This problem became rapidly resolved after my employment of Douglas Williams as an informant.

Douglas was a black man about fifty years old who had grown up in Paul's community and was well known, but not as a criminal. All along he had furnished information to officers hinting at the possible direction one of Paul's trucks might be going. Mostly it was worthless stuff that brought him only the smallest of rewards. He did need money. He had suffered a heart attack at age thirty-five and was unable to work hard. On my first introduction, I told him the only way to make big rewards was to work himself into Paul's organization, assist completely with our investigation in an undercover capacity, and then be willing to face Paul in court and testify. He readily agreed to attempt this operation. Douglas knew that Paul had shot at highway patrol officers and that the only action to come of it was the patrolman being transferred to another part of the state.

Also, he knew that Paul would have him killed in two minutes if his position were exposed. These things did not bother Douglas Probably because he was absolutely fearless and as courageous as they come.

With this potential bonanza, our battle of wits began. We spent a considerable amount of time designing a special type of tape recorder that could be placed on the person of Douglas, under his clothing, for the purpose of recording all possible conversation during the investigation. A few test runs showed it to be dependable.

My first assignment to Douglas was to attempt to purchase forty-eight gallons of booze from Paul. I met him in the woods several miles from Paul's headquarters and installed the tape recorder on him.

"Please don't make any careless mistakes and give yourself away," I warned him.

Douglas left on his first mission. On schedule, he returned. And to my surprise and delight, he had the booze in the trunk of the special undercover car we had rigged. Hastily, we played back the tapes. A bonanza! The great Paul had one big strike against him. We had the show on the road. And Douglas was a natural for the job.

For about six months, I had Douglas regularly employed. He made purchases from Paul and from many of his cohorts. He transported booze, delivered materials, located distillery sites and discovered a number of stash places. All of this went into the tape recorder.

Probably Douglas' most effective tactic was to provide his own residence and premises for stashing booze for Paul. From an outbuilding in the yard, we made photographs, movies and set up records of persons and vehicles coming to bring or pick up liquor. All the while, Douglas became more and more proficient as an undercover agent. Paul instantly knew that Douglas was no ordinary flunky and soon promoted him to executive status. He participated in the planning and directing, all the time increasing our bulging mass of tape recordings.

On one particular tape, Paul made it clear that he wanted to set up a new stash place for his booze. This is normal for it is fatal to the criminal to become a creature of too many routine habits. Douglas took the initiative and set up what looked like a golden opportunity. He suggested the leasing of an old unoccupied farm house on a certain back road several miles from Paul's headquarters. One of Paul's lieutenants endorsed the suggestion.

Paul's comment was, "A damn good place, but isn't there another old house in sight of that one?"

A lieutenant said, "Yes sir, Mr. Paul, that's right, they sure is another'n."

"Well," replied Paul. "Go rent both places and be goddamned sure that you rent it in somebody else's name. If you don't rent 'em both, first thing you know, a bunch of goddamn niggers will move in next door and start fucking and fighting and the damned law will be all over us and mess us up."

All of the participants in this conversation were black except Paul.

Because of the extreme danger Douglas and his family faced daily due to his work with the federal government, we went all out to provide them with all the protection possible under the circumstances. It was frightening to realize how much he had to be left without protection and relied completely upon his ability to successfully outwit Paul and his associates.

During this time I became rather closely acquainted with his large family. On one occasion, while in secret conference with Douglas in his home, two small sons begged for money to go to town and see Santa Claus at a local store. I gave them money for bus fare and Douglas let them go. Several hours later they returned, while we were still filing tapes and making notes.

"Did you boys see Santa Claus?" Douglas asked his sons. "Yes, suh," came their reply.

"What did he say to you?" Douglas asked.

"Uh, well, he say 'You damn little niggers git away from dem bicycles!'"

Douglas got as much kick out of the incident as I did. He was broad-minded about the redneck attitude of the locals. In addition, he had a great sense of humor.

I doubled up over one military experience he told me about in World War II, of which he was a veteran with a fine record. He explained that as far back as the beginning of World War II, the U. S. government had begun to integrate small units of blacks with the whites. He was a member of a completely black rifle squad of twelve men. The squad leader was black. They were part of an otherwise all white rifle company with a native of Alabama the company commander.

Douglas swore that the commander had tried to get the black squad killed in action to get them out of the way. Douglas admitted that the squad did not always perform too courageously in some combat situations, probably because of the frustrations of their unique position. One night the company dug into the side of a mountain in Italy. During the night, unbeknown to them, the Germans dug into the side of an adjacent mountain. Consequently, the first soldier to stick his head out of his hole next morning got it blown off by machine gun fire.

The company commander called the black squad leader to his post and ordered him to take his squad and get the machine gun on the facing mountain. "Yes, suh!" the black squad leader said, saluting and leaving.

Several hours later the black squad leader returned and reported to the commander. At the time, the machine gun was still very active and had about everything pinned down.

The commander raised hell. "I thought I told you to take your squad and go get that German machine gun!" he roared.

"Yes, suh. You did, Captain, and we went over there all right, but them fellas ain't through with that thing yet!"

While using Douglas' residence as a liquor stash, Paul became increasingly alarmed at the extensive usage, and more so because a neighbor was the father of an Internal Revenue Service collector. Paul was adamant in his admonition to Douglas and his other lieutenants concerning the risk of the storage place.

111

Paul said" You'll never get by with it, going in there every goddamn day. Every time that liquor truck goes in there I get the feeling that I'm going to lose a lot of money. That old man that lives in there has got that boy up there in that tax, goddamn, office in Raleigh who watches me like a hawk. He's not as bad as them friggin' ATF agents, but he's bad enough, and I'm tellin' you that you can't get by with it. You're goin' to get busted sure as hell. You ain't goin' to get another load in there, Now dammit to hell, go out and find another place."

Douglas, not wanting to give up the perfect setup we had going at his residence, resisted Paul. "I don't think you are right this time, Mr. Paul," he said.

"All right," Paul said. "Now I'm telling you, I don't want you to expect me to go spending money on you trying to get your ass out when they catch you, because that's your little red wagon. You're gettin' paid to keep it now, by God, if you let it stay there and let it get caught don't come crying on my shoulder because I tell you when you go foolin' in there at your house every day of the week, by God, it ain't long before somebody comes in there. You have to pass all them houses to get into your house."

"Ain't but one," argued Douglas.

"Yeah, and I just told you who the sonofabitch is," Paul said. "And he runs his goddamn mouth too much. I'm tellin' you, them people watches everything in the world that's going in there. You keep going in there any time of the day or night and they'll goddamn sure catch you."

Paul's apprehension was in vain. What he didn't know was that the total effort of the federal government was to protect his stash—at least until we were satisfied we had enough to hang him. He was so nervous that I finally instructed Douglas to cease arguing the point with him.

Then we made a decision to take a long chance. That was to approach a close friend of Douglas' and to bring him in on the undercover action. The location pleased Paul, so Douglas then made his move. I was satisfied that we were making a sensible move. In the first place, if the friend of Douglas' betrayed us, we already had enough evidence to put Paul in jail if ever he was to go. Too, the friend would be paid $200 per week by Paul and $100 by the ATF.

As we expected, he ate it up. But the poor bastard was so scared it made him a nervous wreck. He just knew that Paul would kill him if he were ever exposed. But he couldn't reject

112

$300 a week. We had also promised to keep him from ever being exposed, unless it was an absolute must.

The new stash turned out to be about as good for our investigation as Douglas' expectations. We kept it going for many more weeks and by the time we were about ready to knock it off, the excitement had begun to fade.

There had been a lot of fun and satisfaction in this case. What sometimes started off routinely always got livened up with some unexpected element. Such was the case with Isaac. He was a young agent sent in from another state for special assignment in this case. His wife was eight months pregnant. This became easy to believe after he started a close friendship with the wife of the tenant who was letting us use his premises. She was a dumpy little black woman with wide lips. She welcomed the special attention Isaac showed her.

"Not a black woman?" I asked Isaac in disbelief.

"Listen," he said, "I don't like black men at all but I ain't got a damn thing against a black woman."

Isaac was the man who said he didn't believe in segregation or integration. He believed in slavery.

Isaac and his new girl friend spent many of the few remaining days together, giggling and whispering. Before his sudden departure he started leaving his post in the outbuilding and going in the dwelling with her. His conduct was such that I decided to knock off the surveillance since we had all the evidence we needed anyway I reached a roving patrol by radio and asked for a pickup vehicle at twelve midnight. We packed out all the equipment and material we had used and met our car on time. I told Isaac privately to have his ass on the first plane out of the state the next day. His selection of lovers was not something I would ordinarily criticize but he had made me fearful of jeopardizing the whole investigation. He made the plane. No report was made of his conduct, but he was bluntly told he would not be needed in court.

On the following day, Douglas made one of his last contacts with Paul. The tapes he brought back were not so evidentiary as they were humorous.

Paul made a payment to Douglas for his work. The money was a considerable wad. As he handed it to Douglas, Paul said, "You niggers got it made."

"No suh, we ain't, Mr. Paul," Douglas said.

Paul continued: "Yeah, all you have to do is sit on your ass

113

while us white folks pay the welfare for you. That goddamn welfare...I don't understand it, a goddamn white man, and I know some of the sorriest in the world, goddamit if a white man can get that welfare like the colored man. I'm tellin' you the truth, I can show you some people poorer than anything that ever lived, not drawing a goddamn penny from the welfare. They got to look after them sorry sonsofbitches that don't need anything. I can show you a white woman that stayed here in this county, and you know her, had a gang of children to feed and she starved them half to death, went and got her a home. She didn't get no welfare but all the other white women were afraid their husbands would fuck her or something. She went to the welfare and didn't get nothing, just kept on running on around with every man she seen. I know when one of my men got on the road down there, and goddamn, before he could get on the road good, here comes that woman. Said she just wanted to let him have some. That's what burns my ass up about this civil rights crap, goddamnit, you colored people has just as much freedom as the white people, what is it that the white man's got that you ain't got or can't get if you got brains enough to get it? What is it? Then you all fight and raise hell all the time! Looks like the white man is goin' to have to leave this goddamn country pretty soon. They going to extremes with this welfare and government.

"Another thing! It ain't right that a man runs a place of business but don't have no control over it. If a white man comes in and you don't want to serve him, you ought not to be forced to fool with him. Suppose you run a place and an old sorry assed white man's all the time coming in there drunk and you tell him to get his ass out of there and he don't. You get a rock and knock the sonofabitch in the goddamn head, and see what they do to you!

"Well, I don't want to say anymore about it. I get mad every time I mention the damned thing. I got other things on my mind right now, anyway. I got a sonofabitch down here trying to under sell me. He comes up here and he wants to buy whiskey from me. He cuts it down and makes it sorry as hell and then drops the price. I ain't gonna mess with that sonofabitch for three more minutes. If he don't get any more whiskey until I carry it to him, he's got his last jar."

Douglas said, "If it don't bead right and it looks cloudy..." Douglas meant that the whiskey had been tampered with or diluted so that it was not considered quality stuff.

114

Paul said, "He's got some of the goddamned meanest whiskey down there that I've ever seen in my life. The goddamned sonofabitch sets down there on his fat ass and Jews you down on the price, then mixes all kind of shit into it, and sells it for any goddamn thing that a man will pay for it. A man is a damn fool to fuck with it. I'll never sell him none at all unless it is some kind of goddamn shit that ain't worth having."

Douglas said, "He'll sell it for $2.50 a quart won't he?"

Paul answered, "He'll sell it for any goddamn thing above what he pays."

Cleverly, Douglas led him on. "He's knocking out your profits, ain't he, Mr. Paul?"

Paul said, "Why, he's ruining it! Absolutely ruining it. He's not holding up the price of whiskey. He ain't got nothin' down there but his ass and his hat, just sittin' there in an old house and if the damn law gets him, they ain't got a goddamn thing. The way he cuts the price on honest people like me, I know what they ought to do with him. That's how come Al Capone killed so many people. He wouldn't last long under Al Capone. Here's a man like me having to bear all kinds of burdens, pay off all kinds of law and protect the whole goddamn community. Like Al Capone, then a sonofabitch moves right in under him and starts to cutting the prices. Beer! Whiskey! Or anything! Shit! Go down there and look one of these days and see what happens to him. You may find the goddamn sonofabitch in the river! That may be what I'll do with him. Four or five dollars a jar! Fuck it all up. Jew you down on the prices as cheap as he can and then go make a dollar and that's all he gives a goddamn about! That ain't right. He ought to hold up the price of whiskey. They ain't never been enough profit in it."

Douglas said, "Too much work in it, ain't there, Mr. Paul?"

"It's nothing but a goddamn burden. They catch your goddamn men then you gotta protect them. You gotta pay off all kinda law and pay a bunch of crooked lawyers to get the men out. It ain't worth it, I'll tell you that. The thing about it is, you got to go down there, work your ass off to make it, then when you make it, you got to get somebody to keep it for you, haul it for you, then you got to pay them. Then when the goddamn law catches you, you got to hire a bunch of crooked lawyers, go pay a crooked bondsman to sign his bond, why, if I hadn't made so much money at it, I'd just quit the whole damn mess," Paul raved on.

Paul changed the subject to transport security and admonished Douglas, who at the time was participating in the transport, to be extremely careful and watchful for officers trailing the trucks.

"How in hell do you know they ain't following you right now?" he asked Douglas.

Douglas said, "Well you know, we do it all at night and I could see the lights if they were."

Paul said, "You can't see the lights. Anytime they can follow anybody from Greensboro to Myrtle Beach they can follow you. That's why they can catch you. They find the truck that's hauling it, using them goddamned walkie-talkies. One will sit out there and watch and wait for the truck to leave. Another one will be down at the first crossroads, and if you happen to pass there, he will pass on that message to the next crossroads where another federal sonofabitch will be doing the same thing. It don't take them but one week to follow you three hundred miles, right into the hole."

"One thing, Douglas, I have got confidence in you. I've got about forty tenants living in my houses. Most of them are so goddamned sorry that they won't even cut any firewood in the winter time. They sit on their damned lazy asses until it gets cold weather and then, rather than pick up an axe and go cut some firewood, they pull the goddamn boards off the sides of the houses and burn 'em! They tore my houses all to hell. Sometimes I feel like running all of their asses off."

By this time, by all standards of justice, and the incriminating evidence available, Paul had struck out several times over. Hell, we had enough quality evidence to convict Saint Paul, instead of this Paul. Accordingly, the investigation on the undercover activities was terminated. With this, came the open phase of the investigation. But the first order of business, before our undercover work was brought out in the open, was to assure as much safety for Douglas and his family as possible.

One night at 3:00 a.m. a large rental van truck without lights pulled up to the home of Douglas Williams. I was the driver. Everything owned or claimed by Douglas or any of his family was loaded on the truck. Before daylight, the whole clan with all their worldly possessions were far removed from the dominion of Paul. All school records of his children were personally picked up at the schools and taken along with no forwarding address. Personal bills and debts were written down to be taken care of by Douglas' agent, now in reverse roles. At first

Douglas was my agent. From here on out, I was his agent. We moved the family into comfortable quarters where they would be safe many miles away.

Then we lowered the boom.

One of the biggest roundup campaigns on record began.

Previously, in anticipation of roundup day, I had diverted Douglas and his two ton truckload of booze, enroute to a stash, to a rendezvous with an electronics expert from Atlanta and me in some woods a few miles from his destination. There the expert installed a homing device on the truck which was frequently used by Paul's organization.

We were depending on this truck to lead us to a mammoth distillery, owned by Paul, some 175 miles away near the Atlantic coast. We had to find that still.

On the day before the knock off raids, three federal cars took up positions in strategic places, using two way radios for communication. We were going to follow that truck to its destination, which all intelligence indicated would be one of the largest moonshine outfits ever installed along the Atlantic coast.

At daylight, we picked up the tell-tale beep-beep of the transmitter that we had installed three weeks earlier. We picked it up with an aircraft in the air. We waited. We found it necessary to have a back up airplane because these small ones had to be refueled every few hours. Once the truck got underway, we couldn't stop for fuel but would have to stick with the truck like a case of chiggers.

In the late afternoon, the truck began moving. An instant radio message came from the plane. The beeping noise could be heard in the plane for about twenty miles, but only about three miles in a ground unit under normal conditions. The truck went to the main highway and headed east. Fortunately, our prime plane had just refueled at the Raleigh-Durham airport and got back in position.

For hours, the plane relayed constant directional changes to the cars that followed the beautiful beep. The truck traveled main roads for awhile, then took secondary roads for many additional miles. Then it switched back to the main highway.

Our ATF observer, my old friend Mack, and the pilot had the damndest nerve I have ever seen for this work. After about three hours and over a hundred miles east of Paul's kingdom, I began worrying about the fuel supply. Frequently I questioned Mack in the plane, an agent so calm that he would make coffee nervous.

He assured me that the gas would be adequate. "We'll soon have him to the ocean and I know that he'll stop before there," he said.

"How in hell are you going to make it back to a lighted airstrip after dark?" I asked.

"To hell with the gas," he said, very calmly. "We'll slide this sonofabitch into one of these swampy lakes and beach her if we have to." He meant business. Almost anyone else I know would have given up the project and searched for a lighted landing strip and safety.

In another hour, during which the truck had begun taking more backroads, it went into a large, sparsely inhabited area—just miles and miles of woodland and swamp. Finally, the truck turned off a secondary road in this remote terrain and slowly went down what looked like an old farm road. Mack reported it to the cars, and shortly thereafter reported the truck had stopped and that lights had been turned off.

"Now get your ass back to the nearest place you can set down and find gas," I told him. "We'll take over from here."

Agents were rushed into the area. Individual agents were dropped off at nearby roads. Several hours later that night, the truck was spotted coming back out to the public road. Again, it headed west. Back toward Paul's territory we were sure.

Soon after his departure overhead, Mack called by radio and said they had found a small town with a lighted airport where they set down safely with a "snuffbox full" of gas left. I picked him up in my car. Mack was positive the area last entered by the truck was the general area of the distillery. He and the pilot left for Raleigh to get some sleep before getting airborne next day to monitor our progress in finding the distillery.

Returning to the area, I called a meeting with all the agents. We went to the home of a local ATF agent and told him the story

"Paul Barker has a still in my territory?" he asked incredulously. "I don't believe it." His area normally produced very small rigs not big enough to fool with.

The local agent called his wife and she prepared us a good breakfast. Then we went to the local ATF office and made elaborate plans to find the distillery and set up a raid. Even though we had it in the woods, it would be like searching for the needle in the haystack to find it secretly.

I briefed all the agents on the full knowledge that I had of this gigantic organization. The most important item at this time was that I knew the identity of the distillery foreman.

Paul had hired Clint Mason several years ago to set up, organize and supervise the complete distillery operation. A mountain man, descendant of elite moonshiners for generations, Clint was one of the finest brewmasters in the country. Even so, his most impressive talent was in distillery security. He would string fine black threads between the trees, around the distillery, almost invisible to the human eye. At times these threads would be a quarter of a mile from the distillery, but would always completely encircle the premises. Then, like a trapper, before anyone entered the premises for work, Clint would check his "trap" to see if any string were broken. He spent hours every day foot patrolling. After raiding one of his distilleries, we could see his foot tracks every few feet for miles around.

It was for this reason he had earned the nickname, "The Red Fox."

No one knew of Clint or any helpers ever having been caught at one of his stills after officers found it unattended and left to return later for a raid. He occupied a prominent place on our major violator list.

We scanned maps of the area for a long time, finally picking an approach route from the rear side of the woodland into which the truck had disappeared. The trip would be long and painful. The possibility of finding the distillery, finding it in operation and finding Clint there instead of off on one of his scouting missions, was collectively remote. Yet, we were eager to give it a whirl.

Using a panel truck, we dropped off in the area about 10:00 a.m. After four hours of walking through the semi-swampland, I heard a low but unmistakable noise of a high pressure oil burner used by Paul's men to fire the boilers. It appeared to be about half a mile away.

Guided by the noise, we split into two teams at this unusual distance from the distillery to encircle a very large area in an effort to trap Clint, even though he might be on a scouting mission. We began making a circle, half of us to the left and the other half to the right. Individuals dropped off at the assumed-to-be proper intervals. A prearranged time was set for "flushing" the operators, at about 3:30 p.m. This would give us ample time to gain our positions and close the circle.

We had a very large raiding party of twelve men. Normally this would have been far too many, but in this situation they were quite necessary.

I assigned the fastest man in the party to act as the flush

119

man. He was a young and athletic ABC officer from Raleigh, very aggressive. My self-assigned job was to be the last to complete the circle, then to cover that possible escape route.

The circling was completed just before the zero hour.

At precisely 3:30 p.m., I heard a terrible scream that sounded like Geronimo making his last attack. All hell broke loose on the distillery ground, about fifty yards from me. I heard a lot of scuffling, loud cussing, and then heard something tearing through the underbrush toward me like a mad bull on the loose. It was a large young black man with horror on his face. After a short distance, I overtook and tackled him. On the ground, we had the usual fight. He lost and became a prisoner of the United States Treasury Department.

Quickly I handcuffed him and led him to the distillery. There I saw a fierce fight under way between Tommy, my flush man, and the old Red Fox himself! I knew Tommy would take him, even before I reached him to assist. Clint was finally overpowered and arrested. Two others of minor importance were arrested by other officers in our party. No one escaped.

This distillery was a true monster. Not only was it huge, but very elaborately set up for maximum production. It would have turned out a good product except for the automotive radiators being used as condensers. The zinc and lead in these components were poisonous. This had been the theme of a campaign by the ATF public relations team for some time, the most devastating action ever taken against moonshiners.

Interestingly, the whiskey being manufactured here went into fifty gallon oaken barrels charred on the inside. Paul had gone into competition with the big legal distillers by making "charred" liquor. A term used by his organization was "chartered" included melting brown sugar, deliberately converting it into a syrup, then using it to color several gallons of booze at a time. This cheating brought a double price for the illegal stuff.

Immediately after this seizure and raid, I reached Mack in the plane by radio. I gave the word to pass on to raiding crews standing by in Paul's area to hit all the stashes.

During the afternoon and early part of the night, dynamite galore boomed through this area. All this time, Mack radioed the results on the raids in progress. Gratifying reports were coming in concerning the amount of whiskey seized and the numerous arrests being made.

Dozens of major violators and lesser ones were arrested. A

fleet of new and old cars were seized, along with several large trucks. Two stash places were knocked off along with another distillery over two hundred miles away.   The instant fruits of the knock off included the arrest of ten of the twenty most wanted moonshiners in this case. This looked spectacular for us on paper, since it sometimes required large teams of agents to make a case on just one of these violators, plus plenty of time.

As a last cover for Douglas, and only to temporarily confuse Paul and his many smart lawyers, a bogus warrant was issued for Douglas. This, we hoped, would give us a little more time to further tighten his security. This plan worked only for a few days. Soon a massive effort through many avenues was launched by Paul's underworld to find Douglas, now known by Paul to be his Judas. Private detectives were employed, one bonding agency, one major bank to whom Douglas owed a small note. The ferocity of their efforts to find him far exceeded our expectations.

The normal master criminal would have considered the whole deal a part of the game, or an occupational hazard. But not Paul. It became necessary to place armed guards at Douglas' hideaway around the clock.   Then he was moved from place to place under the protection of United States marshals from Washington, D. C.

When we did eventually go to trial with this bonanza case in U.S. District Court, the "education" began. It was then that I fully learned of the brilliance and awesome wide-spread influence of Paul Barker. Many pieces of advice by better investigators who had worked on Paul before my time were confirmed to be exactly correct.

The gist of the advice was: "Great work that you have done. But to catch him is one thing. To convict him is entirely another matter." No greater truth was ever spoken.

The trial lasted almost two weeks. Paul had a battery of three law firms but none of these lawyers offered any defense and were content to harass government witnesses, probably just to entertain Paul, who sat calmly through the complete trial with no visible concern showing.

Most of the tape recordings and transcripts of them were admitted into evidence. Each juror had a copy of the transcripts for guidance. This evidence, and all other evidence, especially the brilliant job done in testimony by Douglas, didn't mean a damn thing.   When the government finished presenting the mountain of evidence, the defense offered nothing. No**thing!**

121

Nevertheless, Paul Barker emerged from the court a free man.

In my judgment, the trial cost Paul about $100,000. It cost the United States government much more. The most expensive item of the government's tab, however, was not to be measured in dollars, but in the erosion of confidence in the system of justice by the few spectators who understood the proceedings, and more especially the damage to the spirit and morale of the professional agents who worked to apprehend these criminals.

Douglas completed his testimony on the final day of the trial. In a motel room, under heavy guard a few hours later, he collapsed with a bleeding ulcer. He was rushed to a hospital. He was given little chance to survive. But survive he did for a few short years.

During that time, I personally arranged schooling and jobs for his family, assisted him in purchasing a neat and modern brick home, the only one that he had ever had with an indoor bathroom. His last few years were pleasant in these surroundings, leaving him plenty of time to fish and to realize that at least his children would now have opportunities that otherwise they never would have had.

CHAPTER 11
AN EYE FOR AN EYE

The rifle shot cracked with a shattering sqpw-yaeeee. I dropped to the ground and hugged it like mad. Only Reb Estes could have fired that shot on this farm. He owned it through title to a relative, a common practice. We had never seen nor could we prove that he tried to shoot federal agents searching for his moonshine stills, but we knew it to be a fact.

I could see no trace of the trigger man. The shot, like so many others in the past, came from hiding. With drawn revolver, I looked for a target, knowing I would find none.

All law enforcement people called Reb evil, mean and vicious. Folks said the devil grabbed Reb from his mother's womb and commissioned him to the life of crime. He had killed several men in the past, but never had he been convicted. He was a giant in the Carolina liquor business, also being connected with an interstate auto theft ring. The North Carolina State Bureau of Investigation constantly sought him, but, like us, they were never quite successful in building an airtight case on him.

Two or three more shots zinged by but none as close as the first. I lay in a ditch, relatively safe for several minutes, my eyes searching for his presence. I had told the boys that the best thing we could do was to catch him with the right opportunity and kill him. But he never allowed us this opportunity.

It must have been an hour before I dared move on with my search. No more rifle shots were heard. I continued the routine search for his distillery with no luck.

"Damn him," I thought. "I'm getting a bellyful of his shooting sprees. I'm gonna get even with that bastard. He's gonna pay. How can we fix him? Not necessarily bodily harm, but what can we do to let him know we won't tolerate his actions?"

By the time I got back to my pickup rendezvous, I had decided to organize a midnight raiding party. Tonight, I knew where he kept several cars concealed, most being used in the liquor business and probably some of them stolen and repainted.

I didn't mention my plan to the agent who picked me up because he was young and I didn't want to subject him to the type of deal I was planning. Besides, I didn't know him well enough to trust him.

Back at ATF headquarters, I consulted Grandy, who had had plenty of trouble with Reb. "Sure, shoot the sonofabitch if you can get away with it," he advised. "But I can't go with you tonight. I've got other work to do."

Later in the day I ran into Mack, a good agent friend who worked in Reb's territory, anyway. He was delighted. "I'm sure as hell glad to find someone willing to do something to the bastard," he raved. Mack volunteered to recruit several local officers who hated Reb and were willing to go with us.

To damage him financially was sufficient to satisfy my irritation with him at this time. But in such a night raid, which would be done as vigilantes and not as an official law enforcement act, special talent would be required. Too, when you get close, you never know just what will happen. Maybe, if luck was with us, we would get that chance to kill him, a real stroke of luck. That is, if we could get by on justifiable homicide.

I cautioned Mack about the state officer personnel he recruited for this mission. They had to be completely reliable and capable of **"DENYING THE ALLEGATIONS AND DAMNING THE ALLEGATORS"** in the event anything went wrong. Mack was very sure of two state agents. I knew them both and concurred. We had worked together for quite a while and all of us knew too much on each other already which precluded forever any mention of this unauthorized, clandestine, retaliatory act we were about to commit.

Mack and I raided all the government cars we could find and borrowed all the dynamite, detonators and fuse we could muster. We also took along a good supply of ammunition.

We met Hal and Dave in the edge of the city and held a brief council of war. I laid it out. "The sonofabitch took a few more shots at me today," I told them and watched it soak in.

Hal said, "That makes me mad as hell; he's done the same to me twice, and he's too yellow to let you see him when he does it."

This was easy, working these men into the fury necessary to motivate them into helping me do what I had planned. For a while, I thought I had overdone it, as they were primed to go too far. I explained that I didn't want anyone hurt, rather that our mission was to destroy his fleet of liquor cars. Quickly I described their hiding place.

Then we set out with blood in our eyes, each hoping that someway, Reb would get in the way and give us an excuse to shoot him. "Too much to hope for," I thought.

We pulled into a familiar hiding place in the woods along the highway, about halfway to our destination, to wait for later hours and to swig on the bottle I'd brought along. After two or three drinks each, we were even more thirsty for Reb's blood. Someone retold the old story about Reb cursing the Lord when it rained hard and during thunder storms. He is alleged to have said that when he died, instead of going to heaven, he hoped to go to a place where there was nothing but one big whiskey still.

At midnight we departed to complete the infamous journey. Around 1:00 a.m. we reconnoitered at the hiding place of the whiskey cars. They were locked behind a rickety gate and fence complex which once had been somebody's dream of another Darlington 500. This long abandoned country type race track made Reb an excellent place to hide fifteen or twenty whiskey cars, along with a couple of large trucks for distant transportation of the booze.

As we glided by for a second look, I jumped out of the slowly moving car, and checked the lock on the gate. It had to go. We could not afford the encumbrance of climbing over the fence, doing our dirty work, then rescaling the fence. That obstacle could turn into a dangerous trap. The lock was a No. 7 Masters, very difficult to pick, especially in the darkness. A better idea, I thought, was to dynamite it.

I gave the radio signal and the car rolled up to me in the darkness and I got in. "Go down the road a short distance," I told Mack who stopped in a spot shielded by trees. "Unlock the trunk. We need about three sticks of dynamite." He prepared the charge. "Now we need a double for each car and truck. The last time I climbed that fence, there were a good dozen, so let's fix twelve double charges."

In thirty minutes the lethal charges were complete, each armed with a "cap" and fuse.

"We'll have to act fast after we blow the gate. I'll jump out and take care of that. Mack, you go back up the road and I'll call you on the radio as soon as the charge is ignited. It has a forty second fuse, so be close by and smash through the opening as soon as the blast is over. Pick me up at the gate. We'll have a short ride to the vehicles. Mack, you keep the motor running and watch for the approach of anyone. We'll tape the charges to the gas tanks of each vehicle that we can get to."

This would have to be done instantly, as the proper way to use dynamite in multiples is to split the ends of each fuse, ignite one, and spray the ends of the group. This always ignites the others as the sparks spray shoots into the open split, hitting the live powder in the fuse. However, once activated, the stuff goes rapidly, so all hands must clear out.

Loaded with bombs, the government car passed back by the gate and again I dropped off into the darkness with three sticks of dynamite for a gate lock that had to go.

I eased up to the gate and taped the charge midway between the two hinges on the anchor post. This blast would make toothpicks out of the wood in the gate. But who might hear the blast and come running?

I was confident of our schedule though. We should complete the whole operation in two minutes plus. We did not have to wait for the blast once the charges had been placed on the vehicles. In fact, I deemed it highly inadvisable to wait, even though this was a sparsely settled community.

With a steady hand, I ignited the charge fuse and gave Mack the radio signal.

Forty seconds later, a tremendous blast obliterated the gate, its anchor post, and two or three spans of fencing on that side. Before the smoke had settled, Mack appeared with the car door open. I jumped in and someone handed me four double charges with the fuses already split. In a few more seconds, we covered the short distance to where the beautiful hotrods were parked.

"Damn," I thought, "We'll give ole evil Reb something to remember." I knew at a sweeping glance the total value of the vehicles would approximate $100,000.

Like a backfield in a huddle, we quickly ignited the dynamite, using the leap frog system, that is, placing of the first in line, another man the second, another the third. When the first man finished taping his charge he would place his second charge on vehicle number four and so on. The taping and ignition took only one and one-quarter minutes. Quickly we jumped in the car from which we had removed the license plate and substituted one of a dozen from many different states that each ATF car normally

126

carries, and we prepared to flee. "Not yet, Mack, we've got a few seconds, circle the pool," Mack dug up dirt circling the cars. With a .38 I proceeded in. Then we cleared the opening and headed north just as the explosions began.

There is a distinct difference in the beauty of an explosion made on a common place object compared to that made when fuel is involved. The dynamite set off the gas tanks and the sight of each was something to behold—huge orange towers of flame shooting into the night like major fuel dump fires.

There had been sixteen of the cars, but the terrible devastation we had meted to the twelve, undoubtedly blew up the remainder, including the two ton silver van truck parked in the middle.

"That'll teach the bastard to shoot at an officer of the law." Mack muttered.

Dave said he knew of a barn, stacked full of whiskey jars, that he thought belong to Reb. "Why not just let's go on now and burn the barn?"

"Nope," I said. "We won't push our luck too far tonight. But if that sonofabitch ever shoots at one of us again, we'll really fix him the next time."

We pulled silently and without lights into a woods road about a mile away. The whole horizon glowed red from the fire. I was thankful that the cars were in the center of the old race track where the fire could not spread to the woods and possibly from there to some innocent person's property.

CHAPTER 12
THE PREACHER'S WIFE

"I've heard how you and your ATF friends play poker, drink whiskey and run around and I hate to see you leading such a degrading life. You know that you are sinning, don't you?"

This soft and serious voice belonged to the wife of a minister of a large church. She had lectured us and others of my kind many times previously.

"What is it about ATF that makes you agents live so ungodly like that? I can't decide if it's because you are away from home so much or if you are all just a bunch of incorrigible roughnecks who don't know any better or who don't care."

"I guess all of it fits us, Ma'm," I replied.

Why such a lovely woman chose the subdued lot of a minister's wife we could never understand. Face, figure, warmth, personality, poise, graciousness. . .you name it and she had it in abundance. She could have been a fantastic model, actress, hostess, show business figure, or stand-in for Marilyn Monroe.

But because of her image as the woman behind the head of the church, all these attributes were not fully recognized, even by the incorrigible roughnecks of ATF, of which I was one. Her position insulated her completely from the normal designs of flirtatious men. She generated respect and was treated like a lady.

She worked as private secretary for a prominent attorney and was acquainted with most officers because she attended hearings conducted for criminals who were represented by her boss. Too, she sometimes traveled the federal court circuit with her law firm.

On these trips, as well as in her home office, she used every opportunity to play the reformer. She seemed genuinely concerned that my cohorts and I were speeding headlong to hell because of our passion for liquor, poker and women. I argued with her about this, pointing out that I had serious doubts about the reality of a physical hell anyway, and that I believed there was a serious difference in the "sins of the flesh" as opposed to "sins of the spirit."

She always shook her head in sorrow for those of us who indulged in so many sins of the flesh.

It was two or three years after I met her that we both just happened to attend the trial of a group of major racketeers from Virginia whom I had nailed in a conspiracy to defraud the government of a fortune in liquor taxes. The trial was to last for weeks. But it didn't take me long to find out. It started with a telephone call to my room at a prominent motel. Instantly, I recognized her voice. "Where are you?" I asked.

"In the same motel where you are," she replied. "Did you bring a portable typewriter?" I told her I had. She had some typing to do that night for a member of the defense counsel and asked if I would loan it to her. I told her I would be glad to loan it to her.

"Would you mind bringing it to my room?" she asked. "I'm in 709, not far from your room."

I wondered how she knew which room I was in. Probably saw me enter, I reflected. The fact we were both on the same floor I considered coincidence, at the time.

"Just knock on the door twice when you get here," she instructed. "Can you bring it now?"

Picking up the typewriter, I calmly walked to her room. I knocked twice. On the second knock, the door opened a few inches. The preacher's wife stood inside the room in my full view, looking me squarely in the eyes. Her normal conservative attire of business suits and modest dresses was a million miles away. There was nothing between her lovely skin and me except the skimpiest of negligees. No panties or bra or anything else.

She smiled dazzlingly, ignoring the total shock on my face. I didn't know whether to cough or wind my watch. Dreaming, that's it! I must be dreaming, I thought. Hell no, people in dreams didn't look half this good. For what seemed like an hour, I remained speechless. Finally, the initial shock retreated somewhat, and I took a step backward.

"No! Come on in," she said in a voice strangely husky and soft. She took hold of my shirt and gently pulled me in to her room. With the greatest composure, she shut the door, locked it and fastened the night latch.

"Well. . .lll," she said. That word was a long speech to me. "Make yourself at home."

My senses were still reeling at this stunning situation. Then I remembered the typewriter. "Oh, here's the typewriter," I croaked. I set it on the vanity and took a step back toward the door.

She stepped in front of me and stood against me. She looked up at me with the most beautiful eyes I had ever seen and pleaded. "No, don't go. And forget the stupid typewriter. I don't need it. It's **you** that I want."

Why me, I thought. This can't be happening to me. I sneaked a look at her body. I couldn't believe anyone could be put together so perfectly. The sight of her made most of what I should have been remembering fade out of my mind. In spite of the shock, her devastating body excited me almost beyond control. I didn't make a move. Her fingers moved up and played with my shirt near my neck.

Why the hell does she have to be a preacher's wife, I kept asking myself. My excitement had merged with the shock I had suffered. Under the impact of both, my knees began to weaken. There was only one chair in her room and it was full of her baggage. I sat on the edge of the bed.

She looked at me and laughed softly. "Surprised, aren't you?" Now her voice was very seductive.

"Surprised, hell!" I gasped. "I'm completely overwhelmed, stunned. You. . . You, of all people! What is it with you?"

"It's not nearly so much me as it is you," she purred. "I want you to talk to me. I want you to know that I know where your new apartment is, I know your new telephone number, I know where you go. . .I know just about everything about you, because I've been attracted to you ever since I saw you the first time. And I know that you are attracted to me, because every time I look at you, your eyes flash like swords. You want me and I want you! So we need not wait and want any longer. Let's get with it."

Could it be a trap? A set up? Her law firm was representing some members of the crime syndicate which was on trial and against whom I had engineered a water tight criminal case. No, it couldn't be. If those damned lawyers wanted to trap me, they could never use this woman. A minister's wife could never play such a game and let anyone know it. No, she had to be acting on her own.

She sat down on the bed beside me. Her hands moved over

my face and found my hair which she sifted through her fingers. Damn, I told myself, I can't do this. I've got to get the hell out of here. I made an attempt to get on my feet, but she pulled me back to the bed.

"Why are you trying to leave me?" she pouted.

"Well, I just can't. . .you're a preacher's wife. I just can't stay here.

"Don't leave me now," she pleaded. "I know I'm supposed to be a minister's wife, but I'm getting so very, very tired of living a different standard. I want you and I'm going to have you. Now!"

She put both arms around my neck. Her near-naked breasts rubbed against my chest. I felt a thousand little whirlwinds dancing all over and through my body. She pulled me closer and kissed me long on the mouth. Those little whirlwinds turned into tornadoes. I trembled all over.

But I was determined to get away, and only because of who she was. I knew, though, if she continued these tactics a few seconds longer, I'd never make it. An idea hit me. I'd lecture her like she used to lecture me.

"Look, I don't understand this. You have scolded me every time since I've known you about my wicked, wicked ways. And now, here, this happens. I'm not scolding you, but I am reminding you that you are the wife of a big time minister, who is also a Mason, and you have two little girls."

While I was saying this, she lay back, face up, across the bed. The scene had to be heavenly. The negligee retreated far up her thighs. It had come open in the middle and had fallen away. I thought I would go berserk if I didn't get out.

"Come here," she said, lifting both arms to me.

"No. . .I can't. I'm sorry. But I can't." My voice croaked again.

Her eyes flashed. She said sharply. "I'm more surprised than you are. I thought that you were all man but you aren't a man at all."

For a minute, that did it! In a flash, I dropped my pants to my ankles and started to rip off my shirt. For a second, I hesitated. I looked at the beautiful, now naked, body and fought the fiercest battle with myself I have ever fought. Then I forced myself to look away. With that little bit of help, I forced myself to put my pants back on.

As I buckled my belt I told her, "I'm sorry. But I just can't do it. And it's only because of who you are."

"I won't give up on you," she said. "I can't give up on you. Because you can help me make up for everything that I've missed."

I left her room and went back to mine. I had half a fifth of bourbon on the dresser and I took three big gulps, raw and straight. It helped. But there was not enough whiskey in the ABC store to settle my nerves at this point. I knew it would be a long time before I could put this ravishing woman out of my mind.

I felt sure that tomorrow, if I saw her, she would be embarrassed to tears and would probably tell me how sorry she was to have acted that way.

But the following day brought more of the same.

She came by the ATF office several times until she caught me alone Her composure was unbelievable. She methodically informed me that I could take her out that night if I would stay away from the booze. Being the wife of a minister, she had no time for liquor and did not prefer the company of anyone who had it in their system.

All night I fought the temptation to take advantage of this situation. Undoubtedly, she had been promiscuous before. At least mentally, if not physically. No woman of her position and apparent background could so suddenly act in such an about face manner without planning, practice, or some kind of preconditioning and then be so nonchalant about it.

I made no commitment to her about taking her out that night. But I did make up my mind that I could avoid it by getting polluted in a hurry after the trial was over for the day. All day I thought about this and continued the battle with myself. The thoughts of an affair with this woman would excite an evangelist. But the two "don'ts" kept me straight, even though it was minute by minute. The fact that she was the wife of a Mason and a minister of the gospel.

Somehow I got through the day with the same determination to resist her. Some of my fellow agents noticed her overt acts and I suspected that members of her law firm too, noticed something.

Soon as the Judge excused all witnesses, I hurried to the liquor store. Then I had a brainstorm. I figured that if I went to the room of her immediate boss, an elderly attorney, and offered him a drink, that she would not dare to be aggressive in his presence. Perhaps, I thought, if I got tight plus being with him, she would let the whole thing die.

I picked up a couple of fifths of the better stuff and knocked on the attorney's door. He was delighted, no doubt thinking he could pick me to see what evidence might come out the next day. I didn't worry about a conflict of interest situation. I had spent the better part of a year making the case, which was complete, but I had reason to believe that the jury had already been bribed and that we were going to have a hung jury anyway. This can sometimes be a way of life.

The attorney mixed one of those supper drinks. I made quick work of a heavy straight one. We engaged in pleasant conversation for a while, making no mention of the case. Too quickly, I hit another straight, pouring out something equalling a double. Then we continued our conversation.

The attorney said, "I'm worried. I believe that you have our clients nailed to the cross."

"Bull shit," I told him, "You know as well as I do that more than one of those jurors has already been paid off, and you will leave this trial with a hung jury."

His face paled, but then I could see the faint signs of a grin. My remark must have worried him a little, though, as he, like any good attorney, feared the possibility of a jury tampering investigation. At this point, my terrific energy and gung ho personality were changing due to the fact that I had worked my can off for years in that district and had learned to expect this end result when a defendant with wealth was tried. I had been involved in the trial of certain racketeers for jury tampering, or bribery, and had seen the defendants buy the jury in that case, too.

It is incredible, but during my last ten years in that particular court district in which I worked I was responsible for not one single criminal spending one single day in prison. This was the sum total of the efforts of a man who led the pack in work, spending money on investigations and in real effort. In other districts where I had worked, however, it was a very different story.

This paradox was enough to disillusion any agent, especially when he had had a wife to tell him "I told you so." It did little to suppress the inclination to drink heavily. It also ate away at the motivation that made a hyperactive agent tick, so that eventually he might possibly say to hell with the government. It could possibly make him join the minority who sat around and sucked the teats of the American taxpayer. I tried hard to keep my spirit alive and avoid membership in this clique. In fighting

to do so, I still gave the defense hell and worked hard to continue to make good cases, knowing that nothing probably would happen to them.   The booze was slipping up on me. My mind snapped back to the preacher's wife.   I had another straight. By now my head was giddy and I felt like she would avoid me in this semi-intoxicated condition.

I was right. I didn't think she would come to the room of her boss and start anything. But sure as hell, in she walked.

She was dressed fit to kill. With a sweeping glance, she took in the room. She ignored her boss and looked at me. To my amazement, right in front of the boss, she chewed me out for drinking and informed me that she would not go out with me that night. My plan had worked. She whirled her pretty rear out the door in haste. The lawyer and I went out to eat and I thought I was in the clear.

Tense, and wondering what the lawyer thought about the preacher's wife acting like she did, I kept waiting for him to mention it. He didn't. So I decided to say something about it for fear that he would think negatively about it and pass his thoughts on to those who might hurt our prosecuting effort.

"I didn't have anything to do with the way your secretary acted tonight," I told him. I didn't mention the incident in room 709, by any means. However, her conduct during this day did not go unnoticed. They all realized that she was after me.

Instead of firing her, giving her hell, or saying anything to me, the lawyer-boss said, "Damned if I would let a woman rub it all over me like that. I don't go around hunting it from anyone, but if I ever get backed into a corner by any woman, I'll darn sure frig my way out. Why in hell don't you go ahead and lay her and maybe she'll be happy?"

I was astonished. He didn't mention her responsibilities as a minister's wife. And he was an ardent church worker, one who prayed in public, and was something of a lay preacher! Good Lord, I thought, I can't believe it.

The following days brought more of the same, the only difference being that I knew that her employers were aware of it and could care less. I continued to get bombed each afternoon to keep her off my back and besides that, I kinda liked the booze.

When the pressure got to the point that there was danger of the actual defendants in the case becoming aware of this unreal game, I decided to move out of the motel. I moved twenty miles down the coast to a small obscure motel. It worked for about half an hour. No sooner had I unpacked in my new hideaway than a knock sounded on the door. The preacher's wife! How in thunder she found out where I was, I still don't know. I suspect, however, one of my fellow agents conspired against me for kicks. After all, I was becoming a laughing stock and being called dry-codded among other things.

In her presence, I hit the bottle. As usual, this doused her fire. She was such a great Christian that she just couldn't tolerate a drinking sinner. It was against her religion. Besides being frustrated, disgusted and having these daily bouts with my conscience, I was having real trouble subduing my passions. My lectures to her about her very serious responsibilities were totally ineffective but the booze, so far, did the trick. She left with a mean look on her face.

One night she got teed-off and went to a show with my two closest friends. I was in bed at eleven o'clock when she came to the door with the friends. Both of them were tight. I had a fifth of bourbon on my dresser. The three of them came in, undoubtedly on her demand, and talked for a few minutes and left. Five minutes later, the phone rang. I knew it would be her.

"Look on your dresser," she said.

A quick glance showed me the booze was gone. "What the hell are you going to do with my liquor? Pour it out?"

"No," she said. "But if you aren't in my room in five minutes, I'm going to drink it all."

"Where are you?" Damned if she hadn't moved into this motel. I told her to jump in the lake.

She said, "If you don't come to me I'm going to jump out the window." A good idea, I thought, but I didn't dare suggest it to her.

I called the night clerk and told him if the crazy broad in room 405 called my room again, to refuse to connect her with my phone. I lay awake, worried about what she might do. Finally, I decided to go try to get the liquor away from her for fear that she might kill herself. A hell of a note. She had finally decided to join me in the booze.

Probably thirty minutes passed before I got to her room and the door was unlocked. I went in to be greeted by the sickest woman I have ever seen. This was probably the first time in her life she had ever tasted bourbon. But boy, had she tasted this! The fifth was half gone. She leaned over the bathtub and was throwing up like mad. I called my two friends who had taken her out and asked them to come to my rescue. They came and I told them the whole story, explaining that I couldn't do anything with her.

They must have done a pretty good job, because she arrived on the job the next morning and, except for the tell-tale signs of a hangover, there was no change.

The trial was about to end. I suffered through the final days of her obnoxious conduct and survived it. . .intact.

As I knew we would, we lost the case. All this for nothing, I thought. Three members of the jury had been bribed and a mistrial was equivalent to an acquittal.

I packed my bags and left that city like a bat out of hell. Twenty miles down the road, I noticed her car right on my bumper. I'll see how much nerve she has, I thought, and put the accelerator on the floor and left her flat.

A week later, I saw her back at my home station. Some of her sparks had gone out. She apologized and told me she thought I was the straightest man in the world.

No such thing. I had bad back trouble. A yellow streak about a foot wide.

While I felt relieved, I also felt that I was as much a failure as a pregnant whore driving an Edsel with two flat tires, an out-of-date license plate and with a Nixon for President bumper sticker.

CHAPTER 13
MURDER OF THE MURDERER

"Joe, grab a flight out of Raleigh and be in Atlanta tomorrow. We have a very special mission for you. Prepare to be gone about a week."

That long distance voice was my boss, Melvin Goodson, a rising young government executive with whom I had a cordial relationship. Naturally, I agreed. Melvin knew me, my tactics and motivation well.

My initial reaction was apprehension, curiosity. When the big office beckons suddenly, you wonder. What sin or shortcut shenanigan was catching up with me? Where had I failed to cover my tracks? Had I left a loose end dangling to incriminate me? Maybe Melvin had me lined up for some simple investigative assignment, like murder, for instance.

On the plane, my thoughts were of Melvin and my association with him. He was a handsome bachelor of about thirty, very cool. women chased after him brazenly in the little city near Raleigh where he had previously been stationed. But he escaped the whirlpool of matrimony. He had a great sense of humor and made no one unhappy except the many unsuccessful women who had permanent designs on him, and, of course, the multitude of bootleggers he had caught.

Not the least among his superlatives was that of "bank runner." This status is usually assigned to a boy in a group of youngsters who gather at some swimming hole in the summer to play naked in the water. Throughout life, the male is judged by the size, specifically the length, of his male organ. The champion of the group is soon recognized at the swimming hole. He gets out of the water and runs around on the bank to show off. The other boys, feeling inferior, remain in the water to their waists. Melvin was awarded the title after a showing, not at a swimming hole, but in the showers at Maxwell Air Force Base in Montgomery, Alabama, while we were there on riot duty in the spring of 1963.

Melvin welcomed me into his office next morning with a grin

139

and a handshake. "How's everything in the Raleigh area?" he asked. I knew he was asking about the little brunette doll whose heart he had broken when he moved to Atlanta. Melvin had a close call with her. She was a wealthy tobacco queen who worshipped the ground on which he walked.

"She was doing fine the last time I saw her, Melvin. But she must have really given up on you. She married some runny-nosed kid about ten years younger."

His grin left momentarily.

He gave me a desk and dumped a stack of folders on it that two tall men couldn't shake hands over.

"This," he said, "is a thirty-five year old murder case. The victim was a federal agent, charged with enforcement of the liquor laws. Throughout the years, it has been assigned to the better agents in SIS in the hope that someone will solve it. Now it's your turn. I know it's a big order and that time has made it even more difficult. But the Big Chief in Washington wants us to close the damn thing." I spent a week at that desk reading the case files and progress reports on the old case.

The solution to this case was not to determine the killer. That was already known. Rather, it was to find him. So I considered it a fugitive case.

In the early morning of September 20, 1931, Victor Blythe and Stewart Hall, two federal prohibition agents, slipped through the woods to an illegal distillery in one of the great swamps in Eastern North Carolina. Deep in the swampland, the distillery had been found on a prior visit by Blythe and Hall. Hall had examined the mash and predicted it would be distilled on this date.

From a distance of several hundred yards, Blythe and Hall heard the thrilling sounds of the distillery being operated. Silently they crept over the mossy ground. For over an hour, they stalked their quarry, utilizing all their talent and training.

At one hundred and fifty yards, they could hear voices. Fifteen minutes listening convinced them that two men were operating the still. A few minutes more assured them that the operators were the men they suspected and hoped to find. The main one was Solomon Garris, a huge young black buck of twenty-one, who had earned a reputation of being snake mean and dreaded by law enforcement officers.

How to raid the still? Should one agent circle and approach from the opposite side while the other went straight in? Or should both agents run directly in, taking both operators by surprise? They quickly decided on the latter.

Hall told Blythe, "I'll take Garris, you get the other one."

Cautiously they continued advancing, stopping at fifty yards. Now they could hope for no more than twenty more yards of concealment. It required another ten minutes to cover the final distance to the point where they would jump to their feet and rush the operators.

Hall and Blythe glanced at each other. Hall signalled with a jerk of his head. They jumped to their feet and Blythe gave the usual loud yell. Both young and in excellent condition, they quickly covered the distance. Blythe rushed a slender black who ran like hell. After a short chase, the agent tackled the Negro. He subdued him, handcuffed him, took his wallet to note his name, then started to sit on a log to catch his breath, when he heard the shot.

Pushing his prisoner hurriedly in front of him, Blythe returned to the distillery from which he had heard the shot.

The last breath gurgled through Hall's bloody lips and through a massive hole in his throat. Garris had taken the agent's revolver and killed him with it. He was long gone.

The files, and especially the sworn statement of Blythe, glared these facts. Then came an unreal search for Garris, beginning with the instantaneous pursuit by a rather large posse of officers and rednecks all through the day and night and into the next day.

This search led to the home of a friend of Garris, where he borrowed money, and a small rowboat to cross the river to safety. The friend of Garris recalled later in his affidavit that Garris looked panicky and gave the feeling that he would never be back. Before noon next day, the posse wearily returned to town, telling everyone that they had no luck at all. From that day thirty-five years ago until now, the files were loaded with tips of the whereabouts of Garris—in New York City, the Bahamas, the West Coast and most every other location where a bored agent might like to take a paid vacation on Uncle Sam while running down a "lead." The U. S. Government must have spent hundreds of thousands on this case from 1931 until the 1960's, most on running down phony tips that led agents to merry, merry places.

This total effort resulted in exactly nothing. Garris was never seen or heard from again. As time passed, witnesses or potential witnesses, died one by one.

141

On my last afternoon before leaving Atlanta, Melvin and I went out on the town. We had been through a lot together, both in our work and play, and we had a lot to talk about.

We laughed again at the time several years earlier when a North Carolina moonshiner nicknamed Sweet Mash was found at one of his many stills on a Sunday morning. Melvin and his crew caught him and destroyed the still, using up most of the beautiful Sunday morning so engaged, along with fingerprinting and arraigning Sweet Mash. The poor scoundrel was a three-time loser and a cinch to go to prison unless he could get up the money to pay a huge fee to a local attorney who was a drinking buddy of the local judge.

Sweet Mash cursed his luck but said nothing disrespectful to Melvin or his men; not so his wife. Early on Monday morning, a three hundred pound glob of fat, topped by a massive mop of stringy red hair, bombshelled the office routine at ATF headquarters in Raleigh. Of Mrs. Sweet Mash's three hundred pounds, at least one hundred of it was boobs. They wobbled in an orbit of their own within her massive wobble. Never before or since had headquarters taken such a tongue lashing. "Where's the sonofabitch what's in charge of dis chicken shit outfit?" she roared.

Melvin said, "I'm he, Ma'm. What can I do for you?"

"Nothing, you no-good bastard. You've already done too much, ain't you? Done caught Sweet Mash in the hole. Ain't that enough? Don't you know he ain't got a chance not to go to Petersburg? 'Less he can scratch up five thousand dollars for that damn drunk lawyer that gets all the crooks off. I hate for him to even mess with a lawyer that works for crooks, 'cause it hurts his good reputation. I don't know what the hell the world's comin' to. Very idea! The Gov'ment payin' a bunch of fuzzyballed college brats like you and these others, to go out on Sunday, the Lord's Day of all times, and catch folks makin' a honest livin'. If you damn sonsofbitches had been in church on Sunday mornin' like you suppose to be, my Sweet Mash wouldn't be in dis mess. I ain't never votin' fer another damn one of you agin!"

She waddled out of the office.

Melvin said, "Hear that, boys? If you had been in church like you should have been, Sweet Mash wouldn't be in this mess."

"Gosh, did you see the size of those boobs?" a young agent asked. "I'm sure as hell glad she didn't faint in here. It would have taken six men to take her out—three a-breast."

142

I told Melvin I suspected that Garris would never be found; that I had read all the material very carefully and believed him dead.

"What makes you think so?" he asked.

"I'm convinced that the posse caught him in the swamp that first night and executed him," I said.

Relaxing on the big jet back to Raleigh, I let my imagination, mind, instinct and experience fill in the puzzles of the thirty-five year old baffler. Here's the way I think it ended:

Agent Blythe bent over the body of Hall in terror. "Hall who did it? Who did it? It was Garris, wasn't it?" He tried for a pulse, finding none. Blythe wasn't completely sure the big black man had been Garris, but he thought so.

"All right, you nigger bastard," he said, turning menacingly toward his prisoner. "If you don't tell me who it was, the nigger undertaker will drag your dead ass out of here. Tell me now, NOW damn you!" The bore of the .38 along with the click of the hammer quickly convinced the prisoner he had a lot to gain by speaking fast.

"Yah, suh, boss. It was Garris awright. I din't have anything to do with it, honest. Don't kill me, I couldn't help it."

Blythe forced the prisoner to run in front of him to the hidden car, a mile away. They sped to a phone and he called the county sheriff. Then he called his superiors in Baltimore, Maryland. Take charge of the search, he was told. He vowed to get Garris at all costs.

Blythe took his prisoner to jail. At the sheriff's office a large crowd had gathered. The sheriff was on the phone with Central Prison in Raleigh, begging for bloodhounds. Three other federal agents soon arrived.

As was customary, the sheriff selected about a dozen men from the mob of over a hundred and deputized them. "Go home and get your waders, all the high-powered guns and all the ammunition you can carry and be back here in a hurry. The bloodhounds are on the way."

While the men impatiently awaited the arrival of the bloodhounds, Blythe and a crew including the county coroner went out to the scene and brought out the body of Hall. Dynamiting the distillery was deferred until after the chase.

The sheriff was a tough veteran of many years, definitely a non-constitutional type officer as to the fourth and fifth amendments concerning the rights of a citizen about protection against unreasonable search and seizure, and the rights of an individual to remain silent when questioned, especially in the case of another officer. To the officer, this is a mortal sin and a suspect has no constitutional rights.

This sheriff had surrounded himself with tough deputies. None looked sharp, but all were tough.

At 1:00 p.m. the bloodhounds arrived from Raleigh, eager to run. They were escorted by a wiry-looking old prison guard and a shifty-eyed trusty.

"How good are they?" asked the sheriff.

"Good 'nuff to bring back what they start after," replied the guard.

"This is one chase we don't want to miss on," the sheriff said.

He held a fast conference. Men, I'm in charge of this here hunt. I know these people and I know what to do. All of you, just remember, do as I say and don't ask any damn questions. Whatever happens in here, if anything goes wrong that ain't supposed to, or if anybody comes out and runs his mouth, he answers to me. Y' hear?"

In half a dozen cars, they drove to the still location. The guard asked everyone to stay back while he let his dogs sniff the area, especially some old overalls believed left behind by Garris. Immediately, the dogs took off through the swamp.

The sheriff's plan was to relay his men with the dogs and their escorts, who were accustomed to the torture of trying to keep up with two lunging bloodhounds. Three officers kept in sight or sound of the dogs at all times, changing shifts when the dogs stopped to recover the temporary loss of the trail.

Hour after hour the hunt went laboriously on through the deep swamps and into late afternoon. At sundown, the men and dogs came to an edge of the swamp and stopped at an unpainted four room shack. The house faced a rather wide river and sported a wooden boat tied up at the landing. Two of the men went back into the swamp and returned shortly with the sheriff. The sheriff told everyone to take a short walk and leave him alone with Andy, the man of this pitiful household. Andy was an aged black man known to the sheriff.

"What yo' all lookin' fer, sheriff?"

"Andy, now don't lie to me. Big Garris killed a white officer this morning. You know what that means, Andy? We gonna get him and Lord help anyone who don't cooperate with us. Now I'm

144

going to ask you just once. Didn't Garris come to your house this morning, through here?" He waved an arm at the swamp.

"My goodness, yo' mean Solomon done kilt a white officer? Oh, what we gonna do? Won't nevah be safe no mo' fo' a colored purson to go to town. Oh me, oh me!" Andy moaned loudly. "Well, I jus' well tell yo' de truth. He come bustin' in heah all right, and he sho' looked wild. He wuz wet all ovah, an looked scairt to death. He made me give him my money and he borrowed one of my boats. I ast him when he wuz comin' back and' bringin' muh boat and money, and he didn't even answer."

The sheriff asked about a gun.

"Didn't see him have one in his hand," Andy said.

The sheriff told Andy he would be back later and he rejoined his posse. He reported the information and instructed the guard with the dogs and two deputies to take Andy's other boat and go across to the nearest landing. If Garris had reached that landing, he could make it on foot through the swamp to a road that led out of the county to possible safety. The sheriff would take the others back to the cars then meet them across the river as soon as they could make it to the landing.

The plan called for the party with the dogs to fire one shot if the dogs again picked up the trail, two shots if in hot pursuit, and three shots, continuing at intervals, if Garris were captured.

The sheriff took aside the two deputies to accompany the bloodhounds for a secret conference. He entrusted to them a special mission. "Boys, if we take him in, we may not get him convicted. Nobody is left to testify that they saw him shoot Hall. Andy didn't see no gun. Garris has probably already thrown it away. On top of that, they may not hang the sonofabitch if we do try him."

He was silent for several minutes, giving his comments time to be considered by the two deputies. He took a long drag on a cigarette and paced back and forth.

"We been working for a long time boys, and we been through a lot. But we ain't never had an officer killed outright before with his killer getting away. I just want to ask you both, and I know that I can trust both o' you or you wouldn't be here. Do we want to take this bastard in and take a chance of him being acquitted, or just getting a prison sentence, or do we want to settle it tonight?" The question was more of a definite statement. "Remember, old Hall was a real friend to us, even if he was a federal officer, and remember his two little boys. They gonna have to grow up without a daddy on account of that bastard."

The deputies looked long and hard at each other, then at the sheriff. "You mean you want us to. . . .?" one asked.

"Yeah, you get the point. I hate to do it or ask you to, but we got to look after justice. You know, some smart lawyer is liable to take his case and frig up the thinkin' of the jury. You know how it is, somebody on a jury might weaken and let the bastard off. Now we just can't have that. If we let some nigger get by with something like this, we'll be at their mercy. Won't be safe for no white woman in the country to walk down the road by herself. And too, if Garris gets off, every nigger in the county will be wantin' to kill an officer. No siree, we just can't have it."

So the pact was made. In the likely event that the dogs caught up with Garris, it was not going to work for the prison guard, the trusty, nor the majority of the posse to see or suspect anything.

"It'll take us an hour to go back to the car and another hour to drive across to the landing. I'll be thinking of some way to get rid of everybody we don't want in on this deal," the sheriff sounded confident.

During the long walk back to the car and the ride to the other side of the river, the sheriff was silently concentrating on whom he could trust and on how to get rid of the others without arousing suspicion. By the time they reached the destination, he had his plan. He turned every contingency over in his mind. This was new. He had spent many years uncovering the evidence to terrible crimes. Now he was about to commit one and he was totally occupied with how to cover it so thoroughly it would never be uncovered.

The rendezvous at the boat landing occurred at midnight. The sheriff saw that part of his plan would be easier than he hoped. Several members of the posse were exhausted. He took advantage of this fact and eliminated many of them by suggesting that a smaller group could go faster with less noise. Several men volunteered to return to town. The sheriff decided to use only his two trusted deputies and, of course, Blythe. He didn't like having a federal agent in on the deal, but he had found no way to talk Blythe into giving up the hunt. Blythe and Hall had been very close partners. Too, Blythe would never be able to satisfactorily explain to his superior why he had quit a hot chase for the killer of his partner. This didn't worry the sheriff, because he had come to know and respect Blythe quite a lot. He would have to take this chance.

His only remaining concern was how to either keep the prison guard and the trusty from seeing anything, or how to seal their mouths forever in the event they did see it. This worry was real. He did not know the guard and the trusty was a criminal who could be expected to do anything he could to hang an enforcement officer. After all, it probably was an officer who had sent him to prison.

Cutting everyone out except Blythe, his two deputies, the guard and the trusty was easy. He would have to play the rest by ear. He knew that sometime in the coming hours necessary to overtake Garris he would think of something. Already this final phase of the plan formed in his mind.

As the team worked with the dogs and again picked up the scent of Garris from Andy's first boat tied at the dock, the sheriff knew what he must do. He joined Blythe and candidly outlined his plan. Blythe bought it without a qualm. He bitterly hated Garris by this time. The death of Hall had hit him hard and he was eager to kill Garris with his bare hands.

The sheriff held a group caucus. He assigned two men to go forward with the dogs. He picked the trusty as his partner to work with the dogs. When each two-man team tired, they would stop for the others to catch up and take over the dogs. This was necessary as the powerful dogs covered three times the distance of the men bringing up the rear. They ran and lunged from side to side, temporarily losing the trail and then running back and forth to pick it up again. It was an exhausting job, but the grim thought of the murder and their eagerness to catch the murderer drove them on.

About 2:30 a.m. the sheriff and the prison trusty relieved a deputy and the prison guard with the dogs. By this time, each man in the party had learned the hounds and how to work with them. The trail was getting hotter, indicating that Garris was tiring or was taking longer rest periods. The sheriff knew that his quarry was near.

They topped a swell in the ground and left the ankle deep mud for a moment. The sheriff closed the gap between him and the trusty, the latter intently watching the dogs. Silently, the sheriff stepped within striking distance and drew his blackjack from a rear pocket. This blow had to be good. With a powerful chop at the base of the skull, he felled the trusty. Quickly he checked a pulse to assure himself that he had not hit the man too hard. With relief, he found a strong heartbeat. Then he put his handcuffs on the trusty and yelled loudly for the others. His yells continued until they answered.

The prison guard, the deputies and Blythe came hurriedly to the scene. The trusty had partially revived and was able to sit up. His speech had not yet returned. "My Gawd, what the hell's happened?" asked the guard.

"The sonofabitch tried to escape," replied the sheriff. "Why did you bring a damned prisoner that would be likely to run?"

"Damned if he ever did this before," the guard said. "This poor guy was supposed to get paroled next month. Stupid bastard. This means three more years for him, not to mention thirty days in the hole."

Knowing that the guard was instructed never to leave a trusty in the custody of anyone else, the sheriff said, "I'll send the deputies out with him."

"Can't do that, I'd get fired," said the guard. "Ain't no choice but to give up the chase and take him out."

"Give up the chase hell," ripped the sheriff. "No damn way I'll do that. Maybe you can't leave the prisoner but you sure as hell can leave the dogs. We can work them. I'll send one deputy out with you, 'cause I doubt if you would ever find your way out of this mess. But we ain't leaving until we either find Garris or until these hounds can't smell him no more."

The sheriff sounded tough and final. The guard decided he had no choice.

The the trusty groaned and began rubbing his head. "What happened to me?" he mumbled.

"Shut your damned mouth and get off your ass, you no good bastard," the guard shouted.

"I ain't done nothing', I ain't tried to get away," the trusty pleaded. "You all are fixin' to screw up my good time, and I ain't tried to run, I ain't."

"I said shut your damn mouth," yelled the guard. He kicked the trusty in the rump. "Don't say another word or I'll brain you."

The sheriff sent his eldest deputy with the guard to return the trusty to confinement. He felt a little sick about setting the innocent trusty up for an additional several years in prison, but it became necessary for the success of his plan.

"I been thinking this thing out, boys. It sure looks like now that we're going to catch him. We still have a chance to do it right.

148

That is, he may still have the gun and may try to use it. I doubt it. He's probably thrown it away, and if he hasn't, I don't think the has the guts to shoot it out with us. My opinion, he'll give up like a lamb. Anytime there is a killing, you ain't got much of a chance to convict unless there is a corpse. I don't aim for there to be any corpse found, but we can't do but so much to prevent it. If his body is ever found, it is going to have to look like he accidentally drowned. We can't have no bullet holes found in him."

After a ten minute break, the three men loosed the lunging hounds. The trail got hotter all the time. Another hour or so should do it. The grim mission the men had committed themselves to caused a terrible silence. The biggest sounds were the swamp mud sucking at their feet and the occasional splashing of the dogs through pools. On and on they plunged. By now the hounds were running less and less from side to side, sticking to a straight line. About 4:00 a.m., both hounds tried desperately to break loose. This meant that the quarry was near. A few minutes later they heard sounds of something, or someone, no more than two hundreds yards away.

The sheriff yelled, "Garris, Garris. This is the sheriff. You might as well stop and give up. We got you and you ain't got a chance to get away."

"Okay, okay. Don't shoot me! Please don't shoot me! I'm stopping right heah!"

Within minutes, the three men were all over Garris. He offered no resistance and grabbed frantically for the stars.

Handcuffs were thrown on Garris post haste. Then all four men collapsed on the muddy floor of the dismal swamp. No one in the country could be any more exhausted. All looked like slimy lagoon creatures covered with crusty layers of mud and water.

Garris was terrified. His large brown eyes shown through the mud like those of a wounded deer. There was no doubt in his mind as to his fatc at thc hands of these men. Somehow he already knew that he would never face a judge for his crime. This realization turned his terror into panic. Hysterically, he tried to claw to his feet and continue his flight. The lunging of the dogs and the frantic grappling of his captors prevented it.

Then came the tears and the pitiful begging for his life. The officers were not without compassion, but they were determined to carry out their plan. To them, this would be justice, however swift.

The sheriff was reminded by the sight of the straining of the great wrist of Garris against the handcuffs that the final phase of the execution by drowning would be a tough job in spite of the handcuffs and the two-to-one odds. An additional struggle would leave the wrists of Garris raw and bleeding. Assuming the body might be found, the sheriff wanted no tell-tale marks. This same reasoning eliminated the easier and somewhat more merciful solution of knocking Garris unconscious with a black-jack prior to drowning him. Cautiously, the sheriff freed the hands of Garris, taking a piece of his already tattered shirt and making a cushion around each wrist, then replacing the cuffs.

Garris continued to weep and beg for his life. He swore that Hall had drawn his revolver and hit him with it. An examination of his head revealed no acute bruises from being pistol whipped.

Garris was bluntly informed of what was about to happen to him. He was given the opportunity to say a prayer for his immortal soul. But he only offered a horrible scream which echoed uselessly through the dismal swamp.

Wanting to get the thing over, the sheriff grabbed Garris around the neck and, aided by his deputy and Blythe, committed the terrible act they felt they must. The ordeal took over twenty minutes. A more fierce struggle probably never occurred in the swamp, notwithstanding the shackles on the hands of Garris.

Finally, the great body went limp. They held his head under knee deep water for many minutes afterward. Finally, they let go. Blythe checked for a pulse and found none. They were exhausted mentally and physically.

The body could not be left on the open ground. A brief search turned up a suitable hiding place, back up under a hollowed out bank, out of sight of trappers or hunters who might travel this area. Another thirty minutes of erasing signs of the struggle, dragging and work at the embankment, convinced the three that they had done all they could here.

"I'm lost as hell in this swamp, but I do know that north is that way," pointed the sheriff. "And the nearest road is to the north. The posse will be rested and back riding the roads or on the lookout for us. And we sure as hell don't want nobody coming in here, so let's get the hell out as fast as we can!"

Dawn was an hour old when they departed toward the north, all following the incredible sheriff. The men had been without food and with only swamp water to drink for about twenty-four hours. About mid-morning they could hear the distant passing of automobiles on a road. Such a volume of vehicular traffic was abnormal for this area so they knew that members of the original posse were searching for them. Thirty minutes more of tortuous struggle brought them to the road.

Within minutes a deputy drove up in a county car and the men fell on the ground to rest. Questions by the deputy and his rider were unwelcome and this was immediately sensed by the deputy.

Finally, the sheriff said, "The sonofabitch got away. Take us back to town, we'll rest and then carry on from there."

Back at the sheriff's office, most of the members of the posse were on hand, along with a sizeable crew of federal agents, some dressed up in suits like they expected to search for Garris on paved streets. Dozens of questions were asked of the sheriff and Blythe. The only response was that Garris had escaped in the swamp, the trail had vanished, and they believed he had made it to the road and was now fleeing the county. This scuttled a plan by members of the waiting group to resume the search in the swamp.

Blythe convinced the federal men that they should take up the search elsewhere, namely on all neighboring farms near the public road, and all villages and towns in that part of the country. The agents bought this suggestion and didn't bother to return to the swamp.

"Let's get cleaned up, get some rest and meet at my place," the sheriff secretly told Blythe and the deputy, who had been with them. "We've got some talking to do."

After a long sleep and a good meal, the three met at the home of the sheriff. He sent his wife and daughter to visit neighbors. "Boys, you know what we've done. The way I see it, we ain't done a damn thing wrong, but you know that we'll hang if the truth ever comes out. So I'm telling you tonight and I ain't ever going to discuss it with you or anybody else after this, we got to keep our mouths shut forever. No matter how much your conscience works on you, no matter how many bad dreams you have about last night, or how many people question you, we stick to one simple story: Garris got away. He made it to the road and vanished. If either one of you ever talks, it's going to be your ass. Another thing: we can't just stop this search 'cause it won't look right. We got to dig in and work around the clock for a long time, pretending that we are trying to find Garris just to make it look good.

"Cause if we do anything suspicious, they'll go right back in that swamp and might find the body."

Affidavits indicate this is exactly what the sheriff, Blythe, and the others did. A determined search continued in the locality for weeks. Thereafter, investigative reports show that the search continued for the next thirty-five years with no trace of Garris or his body.

When time permitted, I studied and reread the files and came up with an even stronger conviction that I was right. I visited the scene and made a formal effort to contact anyone remaining alive who could possibly be a witness, including the posse. All potential witnesses were dead. Blythe was still living but was hopelessly senile and completely incoherent. It was with this information and a medical statement as to the condition of Blythe that I returned to Atlanta and reported to Melvin. I flatly requested a permanent closing of the case.

While the request was in Washington being considered, Blythe died. A supplemental report including a copy of his death certificate resulted in closing the final page in this long drama.

It is my sincere opinion that these three men succeeded in committing the perfect crime. Nowhere in the massive files, reports, affidavits and sworn statements, nor in the investigation that survived all the potential witnesses, is there the slightest finger of suspicion pointing to them.

Thus, the perfect crime, horrible but true.

CHAPTER 14
THE SHOOTING OF THE JANITOR

This case was a big one. It had taken me across the state and required extensive, round the clock surveillance of a major criminal. I went to my motel room at 2:00 a.m. after quite a long day. The call light was on. I called the desk.

" You have an emergency call from a Mr. Boldt," said the sleepy night clerk. I called Grandy, thinking something tragic must have happened.

Grandy answered the phone. "Where the hell are you?" he asked.

"Where the hell did you call, Grandy?" I answered.

"Oh yeah, I know where you are. . ." He was high as a Georgia pine. But he sounded serious and subdued.

"What's wrong?" I persisted.

"Get your ass down here as soon as you can and get me out of this mess!" he pleaded.

"What mess? What have you done, Grandy?"

"Well, I. . .uh. . .I mean they say. . .they say that I shot the nigger janitor at the post office building. Come on down here, dammit, I need somebody with enough sense to get me out of this mess. They done arrested me for assault with a deadly weapon."

"Well, tell me what happened."

"Me and Charley came in from work about eight o'clock and went to our office. Well, these two black janitors came in to clean up. We had us a bottle and didn't want them to see us drinking in the federal building. I told them to leave and they gave me some crap, so I took out my gun and ran them out the back door. I took a shot at one of them but I wasn't trying to hit him."

"What happened then?" I asked.

"Well, the one I shot at jumped in the mail truck and. . ."

"You didn't shoot the mail truck, did you?" I asked sharply, dismayed.

"You dumb sonofabitch, you think I'm crazy enough to shoot a United States mail truck?"

153

"Well, I believe I'd rather shoot at a United States mail truck than at a United States janitor," I said. "Look, I can't get away from here. We're making real progress on this case."

"To hell with your progress," he rattled. "If you don't come down here and show me how to get out of this, I'll be the one that goes to prison! I know you can do it 'cause you have had so-ooo much experience in getting away with things and getting out of tight places."

He had a point. I had to go.

I assigned another agent to supervise my investigation and left for Raleigh. The long drive back to Raleigh after being on my feet twenty-four hours was sapping my energy. But my mind clicked at top speed, setting up some kind of justification for what Grandy had done. Naturally, it required a bit of fabrication. But by the time I hit the city limits I had a tentative blueprint on the mental drawing board.

I called Grandy at 6:00 a.m. He was half asleep and half drunk. I went by his home and he offered me a drink.

"No, buddy. If we are going to get this alibi so that all the dumb bastards who review it in court and other places will halfway believe it, we're both going to stay sober. So put up the bottle and fix us some coffee."

His wife made the coffee. She was furious at the police for serving the warrant and for lying on her good husband. Never could he do such a thing. There was no power this side of hell that could make her believe differently.

Grandy finished three cups of coffee and appeared to be in better shape. I pinned him down for more details. The details enlightened me on the bigger picture. I had to revise my plans to show the lily white innocence of my friend.

One piece of bad news hit us hard. Charley planned to say that he didn't see anything at all, because he was asleep on the floor—due to exhaustion from physical abuse suffered because of the job demands. This would not do. It would take the total ministerial association, three saints, and a nun to convince anyone that our story was true. However, I thought with a good airtight "stick together" story from Charley and Grandy, we could cause the reviewers to throw in the towel and give us the benefit of the doubt.

There were two janitors and the possibility that other witnesses lurked in the background and evidence that the pistol actually had been fired. Our story had to reflect these facts.

"Well, Grandy, Charley will have to change his story and I'll tell him how to put it on paper," I said.

"What the hell are we going to say?" he asked nervously.

"This is what happened, Grandy. "There was no drinking in the federal building. You and Charley were in the office after a week on your feet in a case, and being administratively conscientious like you are, even though you were dog tired, you went to the office to check on the inevitable backlog of reports and mail. In spite of your exhaustion, you were going to work very hard till midnight, catching up on the government reports, after which you would read all the latest government manual supplements to better qualify you to perform your job.

"The black janitors came in without knocking, even though they saw lights and knew that someone dedicated beyond the call of duty was working late. They were boisterous and very much disturbing to your work and study. You humbly asked them to forego the janitorial work, which you would do yourself sometime later in the night. But neither of them would leave. You noticed that you had put your service revolver on the desk. Thinking they might pick up the gun or report you for having left the gun out, you picked it up ever so carefully. Then it went off accidentally when you dropped it on the floor, perhaps from sheer exhaustion. This undoubtedly caused the janitors to flee. You ran out the back door to apologize and assure them that the shot was an accident. There you noticed one of them jump into the mail truck apparently trying to steal it.

"You went back in the office and forgot the matter, absorbed in your paperwork, when, lo and behold, and in defamation of your impeccable character, the city police came in and served a criminal warrant on you. It was certainly a false arrest. Naturally, this upset you and that is the reason that you cussed out the desk sergeant, the arresting officers and the bonding magistrate."

Grandy's jaw dropped in awe. "You see! That's why I wanted you here to fix up this mess! I ain't never heard such a pack of lies, but they sound so good that I not only believe them, but it makes me think that I ought to run for police commissioner."

"Don't get too optimistic yet. We ain't nearly out of the woods. Charley has got to swear to it all and we've got to get the warrant fixed. What I've engineered is only for the government headhunters whose only job is to sit on their tails until some good

155

officer makes an honest mistake. Then they spend a fortune trying to hang him. In the morning I'll go hunt up both black janitors to see if I can persuade them to have the warrant nol prossed. You stay out of it, Grandy. Won't do for you to even be seen with them. I can handle it."

I knew both janitors and knew that I was in for a hard time. I had worked late on many occasions and had seen them many times. One was a radical and fanatically religious. The other would steal the shirt off his brother's back and pennies off a dead man's eyes. I had given this one many drinks of booze from the evidence cabinet, much to the disgust of Mr. Holy. The hell of it was, I didn't know which he had actually shot at. I went to the magistrate's office and asked to see the warrant. The fat little bastard grumbled and bitched, but finally came out with it when I threatened to arrest him for interfering with a federal officer in performance of his duty.

My hopes got somewhat lean when I saw, sure enough, it was the religious one who had signed the warrant. If it had been the other one, a pint of cheap booze would have fixed the whole deal. Now we had to come up with new strategy.

I went back to the office and consulted Grandy. He was not happy with the looks of things, and was having a rough time of it with his nerves. It was all I could do to keep him away from the booze.

"I've looked all over hell and half of Georgia for the janitor who signed the warrant," I told Grandy.

"Damn, come up with something man. My nerves ain't going to stand this for long," he pleaded. "I know you can do it. Anyone who can calmly sit down here and whip up such a pack of damn lies like you did right off the top of his head is a double barrel genius."

"I ain't no professional liar, you bastard." I told him, half offended. "You should see a real liar at work. I had a good friend whose wife caught him in the act with another woman in a motel room. I asked him what he said when he saw her right there in the room. He said the only thing he could think of,' I just looked at her and said, "Well, goddamn it, you goin' to believe what you see or what I tell you," Man! If he could make her believe that, he could sell a milking machine to a farmer with one cow and take the cow for a down payment.

"But, old buddy, you know how strong circumstantial evidence can sound, at times. Did you ever hear of the guy who had been subpoenaed for jury duty, who was asked by the judge if he believed in circumstantial evidence? 'No sir, your honor.' When asked for an explanation, he said, 'Well judge, it was this way. I live in the country and keep farm animals. One day I was down in the barn and opened a stable door to a young heifer to feed her. At that exact instant my kidneys decided to act. I was in the process, while standing in the doorway goin' at it, when the heifer charged out the open door. I grabbed her by the tail and she dragged me out of the barn door and across the barnyard. There I was! Being made to run with the heifer with one hand on my ding-a-ling, and holding onto the tail of the heifer for dear life with the other. My wife saw me. I could never convince her of the truth. And you asked me if I believe in circumstantial evidence! NO. . .SIREE, never!!'"

Grandy didn't seem to think it was very funny.

"Tell you what my next move is goin' to be, Grandy. We'll somehow find that Holiness preacher that rides herd over the janitor who signed the warrant and have your minister see him and talk the bastard into taking up the warrant. We'll use all the power of the ministry with the two preachers."

Grandy's eye lit up. He really liked this idea.

Baucom was a fat man of the cloth who had reformed from being a state trooper and got himself a degree in theology. Now he pastored a small church in the country. Grandy had not met him in the church, since the only time he had ever been to church was when he got married. He met Baucom as a North Carolina highway trooper. They had worked together and Baucom had a keen understanding of this sort of thing.

I had met him once or twice. Grandy had called him to my apartment on one occasion to minister to us when we were suffering the terrible affliction known as a hangover. Like most ministers, he viewed me, a stranger, with an eye toward the possibility of a new sheep in his flock. "Are you a Christian?" he asked sweetly.

"Define the term and maybe I can answer it," I replied.

"Uh. . .well. . ." He stumbled for the right words. "It's someone who is Christ-like." He smiled, probably thinking this was a very educated way to put it.

"No sir!" I replied. "I'm not and I don't think you are either. Christ-like? Look at you, fifty pounds overweight, messing around here in the middle of the week in broad open daylight, not working, wearing forty dollar Florsheims, a ninety dollar suit, and you say that you are Christ-like. If your opinion is right, then everyone is hell bound because I don't think anyone is Christ-like."

He later told Grandy that I was trying to rationalize my conduct.

I explained our predicament and asked for his help. He was eager. I urged him to seek out the minister of the janitor in question and reason with him to squash the warrant. I gave him the janitor's and his minister's addresses and he was on his way.

Grandy and I sweated out his return. His first two or three trips were fruitless as he couldn't find either. Grandy degenerated into a nervous wreck even though I assured him that it was just a matter of routine to get the warrant fixed. I was more concerned with what the headhunters would do and how much effect our statements would have on the final departmental judge.

We were using my apartment for a headquarters. I got out a bottle and invited Grandy to have a drink. He went at it like an escaped convict in a whorehouse with a credit card. So did I. We got to feeling real good. That was a mistake but it quickly settled Grandy's nerves.

The first thing he wanted to do was get in the government car and ride. So we took off to a nearby city where we eventually passed a liquor store.

"Pull over there, Joe, please."

"No, I think we've had enough, Grandy."

"Pull over to the damned ABC store like I said," he thundered.

We argued about it. Finally, he said, "Tell you what, we'll buy one pint, take one drink and put it up and not touch it until the Fourth of July."

The Fourth of July was about four months away. I thought this was very funny as I knew that you could give either of us one drink and we would follow you to California to get a second. We bought the pint.

Next door to the liquor store was a little fabric shop. I went in and bought a long piece of gold braided rope to use as tie-back pieces for the curtains in the bathroom of my apartment. The clerk put them in a paper bag and I threw them in the back of the car.

The pint lasted about ten minutes. Grandy said, "Let's go back through Franklin County and see my friend Zeke Aldridge,"

Zeke, he said, was on cloud nine all the time, hopped up on any kind of pill that anyone would give him or that he could buy or steal. He operated a little country store in an old building.

Zeke was happy to see Grandy and asked about me. Grandy introduced us. Zeke asked my occupation. Before I could answer, Grandy said, "He's a big shot in the KKK, Zeke."

Zeke's eyes widened and his face glowed. "Damn. . .that's what I want to join. How high up are you?"

Thinking of the gold rope, I said, "Wait a minute, I'll show you my rank." I got the bag of gold-braided rope from the car and brought it in the store. Zeke eyed the paper bag with mounting interest. I played it cool and didn't show him the rope for a while. He followed me around until I held up the bag and just cracked the opening, letting him peek at the contents. He viewed the coiled and braided gold rope and rocked backward.

"Goddamn. . .that must be the highest rank in the whole land."

After that I couldn't get three feet away from Zeke. He kept begging for us to help him join the Klan. He said, "Boys, I'm qualified to help out a lot. Look at that jet plane in my backyard. I just got back from taking the Governor to the mountains in my jet."

"Jet? What damned jet?" I asked.

"Why. . .the one settin' out there in my backyard." He looked at me, puzzled, wondering what was wrong with my eyesight.

"What backyard?" I asked, since I could only see about thirty feet of weeds, then nothing but water.

He couldn't get over the idea of joining the Klan. "Okay, we'll swear you in," I told him. He fumbled with a small bottle containing dozens of different kinds of pills and swallowed six or eight of them.

"Really, will you?" His excitement was unreal.

"Yeah, but you know that you will have to pay some dues."

"Sure, I don't mind that," he hastened. "What kinda dues? You just name it."

"One carton of beer," Grandy suggested.

He jumped to his feet and took a case of beer from his cooler and put it in our car. "Now hurry, swear me in. . . ."

I don't remember all the words we used to give him the oath, but we had him get down on his knees before some lighted candles with his hand on a dusty Bible and swear to all kinds of things, mostly that he would report every moonshine still in the country and every bootlegger that was in the whiskey business. Further, that he would continue to pay his dues in beer.

After the ceremony, he was elated and offered all kinds of assistance to his new organization. One of these was transporting dynamite to blow up the persons and effects of enemies of the Klan.

To celebrate, Zeke got out a rusty old .32 automatic pistol and invited us to target practice with him.

"Where?" I asked.

"Well, we'll start with that BC sign on the bottom of the light pull cord here in the store." He aimed and blasted away. Some canned goods in the far corner of the store shattered. "Come on, come on," he insisted. "This is a glorious occasion. Fire away. You're all welcome to shoot long as a target's left."

We did a pretty good job of shooting up the place, which made Zeke ecstatically happy.

I never did see Zeke again, but from that day on, he flooded Grandy with a wealth of information on the bootlegging activities in that area, picking up every tip he could learn from the people in his store, convinced in the strange corridors of his pill-dazed mind that he was helping the KKK.

The next day, Baucom scored. He found the black Holiness preacher and set up a meeting with the janitor. On the instruction of the black minister, the janitor went to the magistrate and took up the warrant. We had to promise that Grandy would resign from the government service, from law enforcement and go to ministerial school.

It worked. The case was nol prossed.

The head hunters made their investigation, read the statements and knew they could never break the witnesses. They threw in the towel.

Grandy didn't even get a letter of admonition.

CHAPTER 15
JUNE BUG

My pursuit of more evidence against the notorious Paul Barker took me to New York City for a few weeks. There I met several ATF agents who exhibited the same fierce dedication as their Southern counterparts. Perhaps their zeal even exceeded ours in certain areas as they racked up many successful cases against the distributors of moonshine in the big city. Once their big problem was the huge distilleries like those in the days of Al Capone, but most of those outfits had been wiped out by such agents as these fellows. Now most of the stuff in New York City was imported from the South, received by dealers and distributed to speakeasies for a grand profit.

One of these punk dealers who made the windfall profits was June Bug, a self-styled wheel horse in the booze business in Brooklyn. June had been quite successful, mostly because of luck. He had not been caught in three years and bragged about his importance.

One night I worked with the local ATF agents running down loose ends in the Paul Barker case. While cruising down a busy Brooklyn street, the quarterback of our crew, a large man with incredible aggressiveness, spotted an automobile suspected of being one of those owned by June Bug. We put the siren on him and immediately the car stopped. The driver bailed out and ran down the boulevard on foot.

A young agent jumped from our car and apprehended him forthwith. It was June Bug. A search of the car revealed sixty gallons of moonshine in half gallon glass jars. June Bug was handled not too gently, handcuffed and placed in the government car under arrest.

Although June Bug was a good catch himself, there were others who could be de-nested if this arrest was handled right. He acted tough and arrogant. The agents were much, much tougher. The name of the game was to use June Bug as a stooge to trap the importers and the local speakeasy dealers.

161

This required singing on the part of June Bug. He swore he would never do it.

"You'll talk, you bastard," one of the agents predicted.

It was already late in the night when we took June Bug to the huge federal building in Brooklyn, which houses the federal court and a multitude of government offices. In the interrogation room of ATF, we gave him the third degree for an hour with no progress in obtaining his cooperation. The agent in charge, Philip Rosenburg, called all of us to one side.

"We can catch a bunch of people if he sings. We've had no luck this way, so we'll 'try' the bastard tonight. We'll call Nicholas, who looks like a federal judge, and have him come down here and hold court. We'll pick the lock on the judge's chambers and borrow one of his robes.

He called Nicholas, an off-duty ATF agent, who said he would be delighted to hold court this night.

It took us less than three minutes to gain entry to the chambers of the federal judge, where we borrowed a black robe, one of many hanging in a closet.

Back in the ATF office, Philip informed June Bug that he had certain constitutional rights, including a speedy trial, and that his trial would be held tonight.

"Tonight!" he yelled. "I want a lawyer."

"The judge will appoint you one when he gets here," Philip promised.

"Ain't no federal judge gonna hold court this time o' night. You damned people are bluffin' me."

Out of sight of June Bug, Philip went to the evidence cabinet and took out a jug of moonshine. "Might as well have a little drink while we wait on the judge to get here," he said. He poured out a hearty drink for each of us into coffee cups.

Just like down South, I thought. The booze tasted like our Southern moonshine, which it probably was. This will be good, "trying" a defendant at 11:00 p.m. I still doubted it would work on June Bug even though he obviously lacked a little in brains.

However, I didn't know Nicholas.

When he came in, I was amazed at his look of dignity and authority. He had flowing white hair and a very solemn appearance—the most misleading appearance possible I learned later.

This man was fantastic. He had no scruples, no couth, no character and was the most profane, vulgar agent I had ever seen. I learned this in the conversation that ensued. We swapped war stories. One of the agents told how the head hunters (internal security) were constantly on Nicholas. One of the stories concerned a young head hunter, probably on his first assignment, coming to interview Nicholas about his reported contacts with known hoodlums. This young inspector came into the private office of Nicholas, placed his new briefcase on the desk and proceeded to nervously advise Nicholas of his constitutional rights. Nick rested his elbow on the desk and his chin in the cup of his hand and looked the youngster directly in the eye for a long time. He let the inspector finish all his routine and then spoke for the first time.

"I'd like to eat you," he said in a soft voice.

The lower jaw of the inspector dropped several inches and he hurriedly gathered up his effects and hastened out of the office never to return.

An agent led June Bug into the large courtroom and seated him on the side of the defense. He didn't look worried, still thinking it was a hoax.

But when Nicholas entered from the little door used by judges, attired in his black robe and sporting the dignified and flowing white hair, along with his stern, wise and solemn appearance, the situation couldn't have looked more on the level. I would have sworn that he was a judge and would still think so today anywhere I happened to see him.

Everyone arose on his entry. "Be seated, gentlemen," he said in a legal tone. "Please call your case Mr. District Attorney."

Another agent stood up and called out the name of June Bug.

"Your honor, this man is charged with transportation and possession of sixty gallons of non-taxpaid whiskey, in violation of the internal revenue code."

Nicholas proceeded to advise June Bug of his constitutional rights, meticulously doing so without a flaw. Damn, I thought, I could believe this myself. It was so impressive.

"Sir, do you desire the services of an attorney?" Nick asked.

"Yes sir, I sure do!" exclaimed June Bug. Obviously he was convinced that this was a real genuine trial.

"Do you have counsel?" asked the judge.

"Suh?" said June Bug.

"Do you have an attorney?" Nick tried again.

"No suh, but I think I need one."

"Then the court will appoint one for you, provided you are

163

not financially able to employ one for yourself." Nicholas singled out another agent. "Mr. Mullis, will you please act as defense counsoel for this defendant?"

"Yes, your honor, I will," said the agent.

"Very well, the court will be in recess for ten minutes while you confer with your client."

The judge retreated through the door and joined us in the outer hall, while "attorney" Mullis conferred with his client. After the break, the judge convened the court and asked if the defendant wanted to enter a not guilty plea.

"No, your honor. It looks like my client is guilty as charged," Mullis said.

"Does either the government or the defendant want to be heard before the court makes its ruling as to guilt or innocence?"

"No sir, your honor," said the DA. Mullis did likewise.

"Then the court will now announce its decision. I find the defendant guilty as charged. Now, does the government or the defendant wish to be heard as to the punishment?"

The DA stood up. "The government respectfully requests the maximum sentence, your honor. This defendant is a terrible man and should be dealt with severely."

"Your honor, again the defendant begs the mercy of the ocurt," said Mullis.

"I've already told you this court has no mercy," said the judge sternly. "Will the defendant please stand. It is the judgment of this court that you, June Bug, will be executed in the electric chair at the state prison in Sing Sing!"

June Bug moaned and slumped in his chair. He beat his fists together. "It ain't right. It just ain't right!" he begged Mullis. "Tell me what to do! Man! Tell me what to do. I got six little children!"

"June Bug, I can't tell you what to do," Mullis replied, "But I can tell you what not to do. When they lead you into that electric chair, whatever you do, DON'T SIT DOWN!"

June Bug's horror caused him to dance around in a daze, mumbling. You could tell he didn't want to believe this night-mare but the conduct of the court had convinced him.

The judge added, "However, the court will consider sus-pending this sentence on the condition that the defendant assist these officers in every possible way in suppression of the many bootleggers at work in this city. Is the defendant willing to do this?"

June Bug jumped up and down. "Lordy, yes, your honor, yes, yes. I can rat on over forty of them right now. Oh, thank you, thank you." He polished his glistening face with a handkerchief.

June Bug went right to work with unusual vigor putting the finger on all the illegal liquor operations that he knew in Brooklyn. He furnished information on places, schedules, stashes, vehicles and the all-important transporters from down South who were bringing the stuff to the big city. As a result, seventeen cases were made against as many violators.

June Bug got off the hook completely and probably still thinks he cheated the electric chair.

CHAPTER 16
UNDERGROUND BOOZE

The incredible Foster Bunch represented a distillation of the elite from almost two hundred years of the Western North Carolina moonshining dynasty. Intensified harrassment by the revenuers in the 1930's forced the Fosters to develop a genuine distillery unparalleled in the history of illegal liquor operations in the USA. Reverberations from the Foster expertise will be felt as long as moonshine is made.

Abraham Foster, an extremely shrewd old bastard who practiced all the angles of the trade, headed the clan. He had to feed eleven children during the Great Depression. There were no public jobs available, not that Abraham would have been interested anyway. His talent and trade, his inherited ancestral profession, was the manufacture of moonshine whiskey. And so the times and conditions favored him, due to the demand for the product that was not hurt much by the depression panic.

Booze had always been cheaper on the bootleg market, and prohibition made it legally impossible to buy the product elsewhere.

Carrying on tradition, Abe operated in large volume. In the thirties energy was produced by wood taken from the land. Steam boilers were made by hand and taken into the woods along with the raw materials. Abe trained his children at an early age not to farm the unsuitable hillsides, but to manufacture whiskey. All the toughness, meanness and feuding necessary in the business was quickly learned by the offspring.

A code existed which demanded that secrecy was sacred. The Fosters would kill competitors who got in the way. But worse than murder was the sin of reporting on those competitors to the few honest officers of the law. Squealing was solidly taboo.

In 1931, an Abe Foster nephew, carried away by an old time revival, got remorseful and became filled with the spirit. His conscience dictated that he violate the code and secretly report on his relatives. His religious fervor did not speak sufficiently for him to inform on his father and brothers, but it did become strong enough for him to tell on his uncles, including Abe.

167

The nephew, Mark, was loved and protected by his family, including Abe's clan, until his infilling with the spirit and subsequent downfall, Thereafter, he had the mark of death on him, especially after several of Abe's distilleries were destroyed. Mark's singing did not go unrecognized long. Tipoffs of Mark's traitorous conduct were relayed to Abe by corrupt officers and the efficient grapevine of the violators. Consequently, Mark's life expectancy dropped to zero.

Abe made the decision without a qualm. He had counsel with his two eldest sons, Jake and Joshua. The two boys, ages seventeen and nineteen, already were veterans. Moreover, they were extremely dedicated to the code and placed it above their love for cousin Mark. They decided it best be done before Mark knew that he had been discovered.

Mark's father, Cain, knew about the betrayal. He grieved deeply because he knew the execution was inevitable. He was later to become vindictively bitter at Abe and his two sons, especially after his next oldest son burned to death in a flaming auto loaded with whiskey on the way to market when it wrecked while being pursued by a member of the minority of law officers who remained honest.

The logical set up for the execution would be a hunting "accident." Abe ordered his sons to draw straws to determine the trigger man. Joshua drew the shortest straw and became designated as the executioner.

The next day Jake and Joshua went to see Mark, whom they asked to go hunting with them. Mark was happy to do so and got his twelve gauge shotgun. He called his dogs. The trio went to Fishing Creek for most of the day, killing some squirrels.

In the late afternoon, they decided to hunt about another hour. Joshua knew the reckoning time had arrived. Abe had instructed Joshua to use his shotgun so the job would be done with one blast. A rifle might not be fatal with the first shot. It would be impossible to claim an accident if more than one rifle shot was necessary.

Joshua dropped behind and waited until Mark walked a few feet to the side of Jake, rather than in front or behind. He aimed at the spine between Mark's shoulder blades and fired. Mark died before he hit the ground, his heart shattered.

Joshua ran out of the woods to the parked Model-A Ford, leaving Jake with the body. Quickly he drove to his home and reported to his father. With few words, Abe and Joshua drove to

168

the office of the sheriff. The rehearsed story was given to the sheriff. He asked them to return to the scene with him and the county coroner.

The funeral was solemn and with few tears, except for the immediate family. Mark's mother was tearful, but strong. His father suffered a silent grief, knowing that the death was no accident. Abe, Jake and Joshua were in attendance, but said nothing. Even though they probably were remorseful, it did not show. Mark had been a good boy, but the code said he had to be eliminated.

Mark's father had an intense love for the boy and that began affecting him. Although Joshua had killed Mark, he knew that Abe had ordered the killing. He was head of the clan. His grief and long-lasting moody spells did not subside through the next several years. Rather, they intensified. He relied on his surviving sons more and more to carry on the booze business. He had never been a heavy drinker, feeling the stuff was made to sell instead of drink. But now he drank more and more. His hatred for his brother, Abe, grew. The confrontation with officers that resulted in his other son's fiery death, he blamed on Abe, too. He resolved to get Abe, even if it might take a long time.

He pondered how to do it. Another family "accident" wouldn't do. Either he would have to surreptitiously murder Abe, hoping he would not be detected, or kill him outright, then surrender to the sheriff. He brooded for years about it, becoming more and more determined. His heightened drinking fired his brain, eventually generating an obsession to kill Abe at any opportunity and to hell with the consequences.

On a cold day in December, 1942, Abe decided to share the meat from a freshly slaughtered hog with his brother Cain, Mark's father. Abe drove to the home of Cain, parked under the great oaks, grasped the package of meat and walked toward the house. As he approached, the loud blast of a double-barreled shotgun loaded with .00 buckshot riddled his body.

Cain walked up to the still body and uttered a prayer. Then he went to his smokehouse and opened a jug. He drank long from it and sat down to smoke. The whiskey didn't do its usual job. Now his hatred was gone and regret set in. Never again would he enjoy the freedom of the hills because his next move would be to drive his 1940 Ford into town to the sheriff. His wife, Amy, hovered over the body, trembling with sobs. She knew that Cain would never be with her again.

169

When Cain walked into the sheriff's office and reported his crime, no one acted surprised. It was common knowledge, although not talked about, that Abe had caused the murder of Mark, and also that Cain had spent the past several years brooding about the death of his son. He had built up a pressurized hatred for Abe that could only end like this.

The sheriff and a deputy, along with the coroner, went to Cain's farm, leaving Cain in jail without bond. The sheriff consoled Cain's wife, then searched the smokehouse, finding a large supply of moonshine which he destroyed.

By this time, Jake and Joshua were mature men, very active in the whiskey business. Not too much was said, but Jake and Joshua both knew that there could never be any further close relationship with the family of Cain. Especially hated was the oldest son of Cain, whom they suspected of informing on them, causing still after still to be blown by the agents. Whether Rufus, the oldest son of Cain, was responsible or not, he got full credit for betrayal by Jake and Joshua.

Despite the advancing efforts of Jake and Joshua to operate with more security and caution, the federal agents were taking a costly toll. By contrast, Rufus seemed to operate without interference. This fanned their hatred for him.

The advent of government airplanes compounded the problems of all the moonshiners in the area. Jake and Joshua were especially hard hit due to their reputations as major violators. Eventually there was a crisis in their business.

Jake and Joshua agreed that some revolutionary method had to be devised. Jake had nurtured a plan but was reluctant to implement it because of the tremendous cost. After lengthy thought and consultation with Joshua, he decided to embark on it.

His plan was to go completely underground. He was apprehensive about Joshua because he engaged in brawls and drank quite heavily. Though wild, he was never a security risk. No power could make him run his mouth about the whiskey business.

On a Friday in May, 1945, Joshua got in a brawl and beat up two policemen, finally being subdued and thrown in jail. His cellmate, a town bum called "Catfish," exaggerated his way with the girls and bragged of holdups, wild parties, and general happy times. Joshua listened intensely. Catfish talked Joshua into

170

going with him on a binge when they made bond, promising one for the books.

On Saturday morning, they made bond and took off to the nearby town where Catfish lived. They visited several bars and tanked up on beer. They took a jar of moonshine with them in their car.

Riding around looking for trouble in the middle of the afternoon, they passed the local elementary school and spotted a twelve year old girl walking home from school. After talking about "young stuff," they pulled alongside and forced her into the car.

First, they forced the child to drink from the jar. Catfish pulled her down out of sight as they rode out into the countryside and stopped on an isolated road. Catfish announced to Joshua they would rape the child. Joshua did not object.

Both men assaulted the child several times. She screamed and begged. At one point, Catfish put the point of a knife under the buttocks of the little girl to cause her to move. The atrocity went on for two or three hours. Joshua prevented Catfish from killing the child victim. By this time she was hysterical and had lost consciousness several times. He talked Catfish into taking the child out to the public road and releasing her.

Catfish and Joshua finished the jar of moonshine and parted. Immediately Joshua began to worry. Not so much for the crime itself, but for fear of the consequences. They had pledged silence but there was the little girl as a potential witness. He wondered if he should not have let Catfish kill her.

A local mailman found the child, collapsed on the roadside, and rushed her to the hospital. For days she was hysterical and could say little about what happened to her. Finally, she recovered enough to talk to officers, including the SBI.

Already they had a number of suspects with mug shots of most. Delicately, they showed her the photographs. From those she easily picked out both her attackers. Warrants were issued and both men were picked up and jailed without bond.

Jake was beside himself. To him, and he loved his brother, this meant another unneeded setback in his whiskey business. His plan would not require too many people, but he would need a few who would die and go to hell before they would inform, or even slip up with the wrong information. Jake brooded over this as much as he did the plight of his brother. He knew that he would never again work with Joshua, so he turned to another brother, Knox, much younger, but very intelligent, who had lots of potential.

After suppressing a mob which wanted to lynch the two men, the sheriff searched the residences of Catfish and Joshua, finding the same type of clothing described by the girl. Some of it contained blood spots, which proved to be the same type as that of the girl. A large knife was found in the butter churn at the home of Catfish and it fitted her description of the weapon. The point of the knife contained specks of dried blood.

In July, 1945, the two animals were brought to trial. Both pleaded not guilty and were represented by the best lawyers that whiskey money could employ. However, the defense didn't have a chance. The little girl testified like a trooper. After three days of legal process, both men were found guilty. The jury did not recommend mercy. The tough judge pronounced sentence on July 14, 1945 for both to be executed in the gas chamber at North Carolina Central Prison in Raleigh.

Appeals were filed, but were ineffective all the way to the State Supreme Court. Execution was set for November, 1945.

The results distressed Jake, who had spent a fortune defending Joshua. His criminal mind was bitter at the state and he wished he could do something more. Though the fate of Joshua was paramount in his mind, he still was obsessed with his plan to come up with an organization that would win the battle with the feds and make him a richer man.

For a week before the execution, the family held prayer meetings for Joshua. No discussion could produce any idea for stopping the execution. On the eve of it, the family concluded that Joshua would die and they could do no more about it. The Governor had refused to intervene. There was never a thought that Joshua deserved his fate; rather that the state was murdering him.   On the fateful morning, the sheriff went to the capital to witness the execution. Also in attendance was a state highway patrolman who later became an ATF agent. Several years later, he related the events to me. At 9:25 a.m., the two condemned men were brought to the death room. Joshua was outwardly calm, but Catfish had to be dragged. He violently cursed everyone. He declined counsel with the chaplain and gave all judges, lawyers, officers and especially the state, hell. He even cursed the poor little girl who was the victim of his savagery.

The death compartment of the State of North Carolina was equipped with two large chairs, situated side by side. The men were placed in them and strapped at the wrists and ankles. At 9:35 a.m., the cell was cleared, and at 9:42 the warden pulled the lever dropping the deadly cyanide pills into the waiting acid. Both men held their breaths as long as possible. Then breath had to come. Both thrashed and strained against the straps. Cords stood out on their necks and urine saturated their upper trousers. After several minutes, the bodies went limp. The prison doctor pronounced both men dead.

Relatives claimed the bodies. Jake and his brothers buried Joshua in a family cemetery back home. They erected a stone with a horrible comment on it about the state.

Jake didn't need further motivation to be a criminal. Immediately, he set out with renewed vigor to develop an organization to top any in the history of the booze business.

Jake refined his plans to go underground. Distilleries in open woods, though periodically successful, were quite vulnerable to roving agents, aircraft and even hunters. Importantly, he wanted to avoid any mutual knowledge of his operations with others in the business. He cared nothing for them and wanted desperately to avoid any liaison with them. He knew that competitive jealousy often caused information to be given officers. Crystallizing in his mind was a radical and complete departure from the age-old routine that his ancestors had practiced. It included a resolution that he would not even tip off fellow bootleggers if he became aware that officers were hot on their trail.

His younger brother Knox, skilled and a fast learner, would be worthy of the plan, for he had intelligence like that of his brother. Their plan would provide for not only the establishment of a monstrous underground distillery with push button control, but a distribution system that provided for a very few widely dispersed brokers. The transporters would be relatives, eternally trustworthy, as their ancestors were. Each would be intimately known and trusted. Even so, Jake and Knox spent months picking just the right relatives and assigning them to special jobs. A wide geographical area, sometimes two or three counties, was assigned to one broker. All customers, dealers or consumers in that area had to order booze through the broker. No matter how long a customer had known Jake, nor how much previous business they had transacted, hereafter he would purchase his booze through the broker, with never a mention or hint of Jake, Knox or the Foster family.

173

Thurman was the oldest son of Cain, the son suspected of informing on Jake's operations. Knox hated him with a purple passion. This was the only flaw in the professional conduct of Knox during the groundwork for his underground installations. He could not get Thurman out of his thoughts. Thurman was a threat, a weakness, a liability which had to be eliminated. Thurman was a very large moonshiner himself, but it was out of the question for Knox to report him. Such was the heritage of the family of Abraham Foster. Kill him, yes, report him, never.

Jake continued to operate his now old fashioned monster still and he was making a fortune with it. One day the feds blew it to the treetops and this was when Knox decided to act against Thurman. There could be no doubt that Thurman was responsible.

That summer night he took his automatic twelve gauge shotgun, filled a pocket with .00 buckshot and drove to the vicinity of Thurman's home at the old Cain Foster home place. He parked his pickup half a mile away and walked to the premises. He knew that Thurman would emerge just after dawn to drive to his own distillery.

At 6:00 a.m., Thurman came from the house and got in his pickup. Knox assumed a position where he could get a good shot from the rear through the window of the truck at about shoulder blade height.

Knox was only about fifty feet from the truck as it passed his concealment in the brush alongside the drive. He fired one shot at the base of the neck and upper portion of Thurman. His aim was slightly low and the charge hit the metal just below the rear window of the pickup.

Now .00 buckshot from a twelve gauge shotgun at close range seldom leaves survivors. Eight slugs passed through the metal and window and entered the body of Thurman. None struck his heart, but they penetrated his lungs and upper torso.

Knox fled without checking to see if Thurman was dead, but assuming that he was.

The blast brought Thurman's wife, a son, and a neighbor, who found him slumped over the wheel and bloody as a slaughtered beef. They rushed him to the hospital with blood spewing from his mouth and nose.

Doctors performed immediate surgery but held little hope for his recovery. Several of the slugs were removed, but two had to be left for they were too close to the heart. Most of the slugs

174

were removed from his front side. They had literally gone through him.

After a long fight for his life, Thurman recovered. By any standard, this was a miracle. Many years later, I became acquainted with Thurman, still a big wheel in the whiskey business. He took off his shirt and showed me the scars on his chest which were made by the slugs being removed.

My meeting with Thurman came on the same day I became somewhat acquainted with the widow of Abe. I left a government auto and walked around the edge of her barn to search for signs of a possible distillery on the premises. I saw none, but I ran into her as she worked in a stable in the barn.

She was known to be an active church worker, but on this day, her religious attributes did not show. Knowing who I was and that I was one of the federal agents stationed there, she said, "What the goddamn hell are you doing here, you sonofabitch?"

"Looking for a still, Ma'm," I replied.

"You won't find one here, you dirty bastard, so get your ass off my property," she said.

Some pillar of the church, I thought.

Knox was never picked up for the shooting of Thurman. The sheriff probably suspected it, but considered it another act in a bunch of feuding moonshiners. Knox was more relaxed now and he applied himself fully to helping Jake with his master plan.

Jake knew the homemade equipment used for the traditional distilleries could not be considered in his new operation. About the type of still handed down through the generations, he knew everything. But for the sophisticated plant that he visualized, he knew nothing. He knew far better than to ask for help from anyone. He had a female cousin who had attended North Carolina State College for one year. Of this she had been extremely proud and had once stated that State College offered almost anything in the engineering field, probably hoping that her brothers and cousins would consider giving up the booze business and learn a trade. Jake had jokingly asked her if the school taught the students how to make more and better booze. She replied that the library undoubtedly had books giving detailed instructions for the legal distilling industry.

Jake remembered this and could see an answer to his number one problem. He had to get the books that would teach him how to make the complex distillery to suit his plan. Though he had many friends who had contact with State College students, he could not go this route. The book had to be stolen in complete secrecy. With Knox he started making plans to burglarize the college library in search of such books. Trusting no one else, he and Knox would have to take this personal risk.

They drove to Raleigh, one hundred and fifty miles away, to case the school, spending a day looking over the place and locating the library. Walking around the building, they made notes of all possible means of entry. They saw few guards throughout the campus.

Jake was not too worried about getting in and out but was more concerned about how to find the specialized book once inside. They would just have to take a chance.

Jake also knew that someone with a keen knowledge of electric power and the installation of the many electric facilities was essential. He had no such capability nor would he trust anyone who did have this training. Thus, he enrolled in a correspondence course in electrical engineering. He dug into it with a fury. Day and night he worked on it, impatient for new materials to arrive. He completed it in half the normal time, making all "A's" and receiving through the mail, several offers of jobs, which he ignored.

Now it was time to get the books from State College library. With Knox he made more trips to case the place. Finally, he went into the library, posing as a student, and asked for books on distillation. He watched the librarian bring back a copy of Chemistry and Tchnology of Wines and Liquors" by Herstein and Jacobs, second edition. Quickly Jake scanned the pages and found the book to be a bonanza of knowledge on exactly what he wanted. This was beyond his wildest dreams. Here it was, all of it. The book was complete in all phases of distillation from raw materials to scaled blueprints of the most elaborate, automatic distillery. There were even drawings laying out all the electric necessities. These he could assimilate as well as a graduate electrical engineer due to the correspondence course.

Jake's judgment continued flawless. The book set him on fire, but he knew better than to get hasty and steal it without a perfect plan. He needed three men to pull it off. Knox, of course, was one. He would drive Knox and another man to the campus, drop them off at the right place, then pick them up after the theft.

This other man was Caleb, his brother-in-law. Caleb had been an important man in Jake's organization for years and had always come through in every tight situation. After several detailed strategy sessions, Jake decided it was time to act.

On a hot June night in 1951, the three drove to Raleigh. Their car had a fictitious license plate, one of many used by Jake. They arrived about midnight and made one patrol around the campus. Then they found a hiding place in some woods and waited until 2:00 a.m. Jake dropped off Knox and Caleb near the campus then went back to the hiding place.

Knox and Caleb quickly worked their way to a window on the west side of the building offering easiest access. Wearing black clothes, they entered like professional burglars. Knox quickly found the rack from which he had seen the librarian retrieve the book. With a penlight, the search began. Never had they seen so many books in their lives. Within thirty minutes, the precious book was found. They made a smooth exit, so smooth they knew their break-in likely never would be discovered.

Jake picked them up on schedule. "Did you get it?" he asked excitedly. Knox took the book from under his shirt. Jake shouted with glee, rare for this unemotional man.

For three weeks Jake kept himself locked in his den, pouring through the wealth of data in the book an average of twelve hours a day. He kept at it until he was confident he knew exactly how to construct the distillery down to the most minute detail. His knowledge of electrical engineering advanced even further.

Satisfied now that the distillery could be built just as he had dreamed it, he set about to complete the personnel in his organization. For several days, he, Knox and Caleb pondered over the names of those to include. Most would come from his old organization, since they were tried and proven. The biggest problem was selecting brokers to handle distribution in a multi-state area. This would be his weakest link. For that reason, he spent more and more time on selecting brokers. Finally, he was sure that his organization was almost airtight. Almost! His greatest worry was a large operator in two counties in the southern part of the state. He had to use this man, well entrenched, as a broker to avoid open competition with him. Apprehensively, he included him.

Then Jake looked for a farm that had all the necessary elements for this gigantic operation. He and Knox scouted for weeks until a suitable one was located. He sent a trusted cousin as envoy, with a large paper bag full of money, over $30,000, to the owner and proposed a purchase. The farmer who owned the land had never seen so much money and quickly accepted.

This farm was titled in a fictitious name and Jake moved a member of the organization on the farm where he resided for over a year before another move was made. This was to test the mood of the community and find out if there were any nosey bastards around. At the end of this period, Jake was satisfied. He moved his bulldozer in and constructed a large fishpond. No spectators appeared to watch the work. When the pond was finished, a large hole was pushed out about ten feet deep and roughly the size of a basketball court. All water pipe, electric cables, exhaust ducts and an emergency escape tunnel were provided for. Working at night, they poured the floor and walls with reenforced cement.

Thereafter, the distillery components were placed in the underground room. Treated beams were placed across the roof, then four-inch-thick timbers completed the roof structure, all water-proofed. Two feet of sod was packed over the top. Trees were planted and grass sown and a trap door entrance was concealed in a small hog house. The opening of the trap door, covered with straw, revealed the concrete steps leading into the fabulous set-up.

The distillery was powered by an electric furnace. Vats were of stainless steel, a far cry from the rough pine vats and metal barrels used throughout the area. Motorboat propellers were installed into each vat with a protruding pulley on the outside, requiring only a belt and a small electric motor to stir the mash in seconds.

Jake had personally done the electrical installations, which included a bypass of the electric power meter on the farmhouse. He wanted no telltale increase in electric power usage on record. Everything was electric and pushbutton, requiring only one man. Three would have been required on an old type of this capacity. This meant two less men to be trusted and watched. The outfit was a masterpiece of engineering art.

In June, 1953, it went into operation. Abruptly the average of two distilleries of Jake's being seized per month by federal agents ceased. All the agents were puzzled. They knew Jake would never get out of the business until the day he died. Yet, month after month, they were unable to find any trace of his being in the whiskey business.

The broker system worked like a charm. Customers by the score throughout the state were getting an even better product through the brokers. And the brokers handled it all.

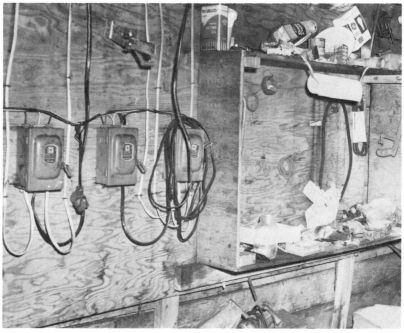

179

Jake and Knox apparently had vanished.

They had averaged a net income of about $200,000 per year in the woods and were never satisfied with such peanuts. Now the profits quadrupled. Jake's cunning saved him in many ways, including not making the common mistake of showing too much prosperity. He lived in a middle class house and owned a farm on which he raised cattle. He made no trips and did not indulge in any of the luxuries that he could well have afforded.

Federal agents were frustrated. The seizure of large distilleries belonging to Jake and Knox had added much to the valuable statistics so important to the ATF hierarchy. Now the absence of that caused concern. Determined agents knew something radical had happened. But what?

Finally, in desperation, the ATF brought in Keith, a keen criminal investigator specialist in major violators. He made contact with an informer who pretended to know something about the organization.

His next tactic was to break into Jake's home and search for records, data or anything that might prove enlightening on the mystery. He discovered a night when Jake and his family would be gone to the State Fair. The informer agreed to participate in the burglary.

After boozing a while to bolster his courage, Keith and the informer went to Jake's house. They broke a window on the backside and gained entry to a kitchen closet. As Keith opened the closet door to the interior of the house, the whole place lit up like a White House Christmas tree. The radio and television set snapped on at full volume. Some whistles were sounding. Floodlights brilliantly illuminated the grounds. This automatic burglar alarm system was a product of electrical ingenuity, namely Jake's.

Keith panicked and did the very worst thing. He drew his revolver and fired a shot, which struck the informer squarely in the ass. Jake had no nearby neighbors. That's all that saved the two men. They were not detected or challenged but they did leave the premises like a chaplain hunting a foxhole during an air raid.

The informer bled profusely. Keith did not dare take him to the hospital, knowing that all gunshot wounds had to be reported. He remembered an old friend, a physician in a nearby city, who had lost his license. There he drove and woke up the friend. The informer was weak from loss of blood. Luckily the bullet hit flesh only and didn't penetrate deeply. The old doctor gave him pain drugs and dressed the wound.

All this was known by only a few people, not even in the ATF, at the time. Never had Keith been so shook up. He scrapped his idea of burglary to get the goods on Jake. Anyway, he would never have found anything in the house, for all Jake's' records were in the secret safe.

Success multiplied for the subterranean bootleggers. The production of quality booze from the new distillery exceeded all expectations. This operation continued for five years and more. The average life of an ordinary distillery in the open country in this area was three weeks. Jake and Knox must have made millions on this one distillery. And with absolutely no income taxes on their fortunes.

Jake religiously followed his practice of staying behind the scenes. Never, during all these years, did he become involved in anything that would point a finger at himself. His broker program worked splendidly. But he still worried about one, a mean sonofabitch, too ambitious, greedy and demanding. Also, this broker placed the pleasure of drinking and women high in his life style. This man, the only weak link in the system, occasionally caused Jake to lose sleep.

About two years after the underground distillery went into operation, I began my rookieship with ATF in that area. For two whole years, I didn't even hear the name of Jake Foster mentioned. By this time, older agents had written him off as being out of the business. Other bootleggers never reported him because they didn't know what he was doing.

It was after my departure from that area to a faraway post on the Atlantic coast, that a woman reported the distillery. At this time, it had operated for over five years. Agents went to the specified farm and made a search. They spent hours searching without success. Trees had been set out over the top of the underground location and they blended so naturally with the surroundings that no one would have suspected anything amiss. The agents gave up, assuming that the woman had given them a bum steer. Never could they have realized that they had walked over the top of the distillery.

This search upset Jake tremendously. He ordered operations stopped. Immediately he suspected a report had been made. Also, he knew that the weak link broker had been fooling around with a woman in this neighborhood. But he could not understand how she possibly could know about the underground illicit still. He decided to cease operation for several weeks to see if the agents returned.

Two years earlier, he had begun provisions for this very emergency, having purchased a two hundred acre farm eighty miles to the south. Already he had a cousin living on the farm, testing the mood and habits of the community. Everything looked quite favorable there.

A second time the agents received a letter from the woman,

scolding them for being so stupid they could not find a distillery. Again they searched, finding nothing.

Aware of the second search, Jake let the distillery lie idle while he worked overtime on the new one on the farm to the south. In a few weeks, he ordered operations resumed at the first underground distillery to meet the constant demand for his product from the brokers.

The woman informant decided to try one more time and fired another letter to the agents. This time during the search, an enterprising young agent strolled into the hog pen and kicked back the straw. At once he saw the trap door. With mounting excitement, he raised it and saw the concrete steps.

The jig was up with this rig.

Throughout the ATF officialdom, this distillery was discussed for months and years. Never before had such an elaborate one been even imagined. Agents from all over the nation were allowed to travel to the scene and view it for training purposes. And it had been located in an area saturated with law enforcement, boasting more federal agents than any comparable territory anywhere—and not a one of them had ever dreamed of such a scheme.

For a long time, Jake wasn't suspected. Officers knew nothing of his proficiency in electronics. The investigation took off on the theory that an electrician would have been hired to do the work. But no such person was ever found.

Now Jake further pondered the suspect broker to the south. His name was Manley Burleson. He appeared to be more and more jealous because Jake always had plenty of booze to sell through him, even when no one else had any because of law enforcement pressure, bad weather, or other reasons. Still, Jake regularly had the same quality stuff. It was good for Burleson, but he couldn't figure it out. And he wanted to get more out of this lucrative operation than just a mere broker's markup.

Just after the seizure, he propositioned Jake, using a bluff, and demanding a full partnership in the operation. Already Jake was half a mind to have Burleson knocked off, knowing that he had caused the first underground operation to be exposed. As usual he was right. Burleson had been shacking up with the woman letter writer, who was also chummy with the tenant on the farm where the super outfit was located. This tenant either ran his mouth or she visited him at the farm and saw enough to conclude that something big was underway there.

Burleson's mistake doomed him. Jake told Knox to kill him. A simple method was devised.

Burleson liked to stunt around on the lake with a high speed motorboat and had a reputation for flagrant recklessness. Knox sometimes accompanied him to drink booze and fish some. One afternoon while in the boat with him, Knox knocked Burleson in the back of the head with a heavy wrench. Then he threw him overboard and overturned the boat. He pretended to dive for the body of Burleson just in case anyone had been watching. Then he swam ashore, walked to a nearby road, flagged a motorist and told the story of the boat accident, overturning and drowning.

An hour later, the rescue squad fished the body from the bottom. Neither the coroner nor anyone else was surprised at the bruise on Burleson;s head. The verdict was accidental drowning. Knox went home and reported to Jake, who was pleased but unemotional as usual.

With construction of the new underground distillery completed, it now became necessary to select a new broker for this prolific area. They picked a longtime bootlegger named Burris, whom Jake trusted as much as he did anyone. Burris became established into this part of the organization, but as was the case with all the brokers and subordinates, he never knew the location or secrets of the distillery.

Operation of the new and bigger underground distillery began about the time of the death of Burleson.

This distillery operated an unbelievable nine years!

During that period of time, the only close call was an accidental sighting of a truck leaving the premises by two sheriff's deputies. The truck, enroute to Burris, the replaced broker, carried several hundred gallons of booze. The driver bailed out and escaped on foot. The fictitiously registered vehicle could not be traced. Drivers always wore gloves, leaving no fingerprints. Jake shut down the distillery for a month and then resumed daily operations.

It was about this time that I was assigned to investigate Jake and Knox. The government had never given up on the possibility that in some way they were still active. This seizure of the truck with the booze was a good starting place, so it was there I began to look into it. There, also, I was reunited with an old friend, Rick, from near Raleigh. We had a lot of fun on the case.

We brainstormed ideas to lead us to what we now believed was a gigantic liquor operation owned by Jake and Knox. Rick told me about an informer who had been telling him that he bought large amounts of whiskey from Burris and that this source was always consistent and reliable despite the weather and occasional saturation raids by the ATF which dried up whiskey for everyone else. The informer, likewise puzzled, suggested that he could bleed information from Burris, gradually, without his realizing it. Rick arranged for me to meet the informer, Mike Rush.

We decided to give Mike the works. But first, we had to use him on a large operation completely separate from that of Jake. Logical, because, in the likely event that he missed with Jake, we might never get such an opportunity again. More importantly, it would give him a good tryout before putting him in the big leagues.

Two weeks later, Rick told me he had it going. Mike had a fix on a large group of major violators. practically in his pocket, who had been chased out of the mountains by the hard-charging ATF crews, who were now applying terrific pressure on all moonshiners with the exception of Jake's organization of which they still knew nothing. Rick arranged a midnight meeting with Mike in a remote section of the county.

Mike appeared driving a hot rod liquor car. Even as I met him in the semi-darkness I knew he was an unusual character. He had a barrel chest and the features of a genuine he-man. He explained his lateness due to having a few barns to burn. He turned out to be the leader of the local chapter of the United Klans of America, the infamous KKK. He spent thirty minutes telling Rick what he had done this night. It included burning two outbuildings on two separate farms. One victim was punished for being a nigger lover, and the other for inadequately supporting his family. The latter man spent his money on booze while his wife and kids went hungry. It didn't occur to Mike that the man's booze could be some of that which he was selling.

We didn't talk about Jake's organization on this first meeting.

He laid out the other large operation and stated he knew the distillery location. Rick dropped Mike and me off in the darkness some twenty minutes away and on foot we went to a farm he designated. Sure enough, it was there. I examined the premises and in spite of the annoying barking of dogs, I broke into the barn and found an enormous distillery, complete with steam boilers and all the works. We rejoined Rick and reported our findings.

Mike, said, "Rick, I like this guy very much. I'll tell you right now. He knows what he's doing. I'll tell you something else, too. If he lets me down, I'll cut his damned heart out and send it to you by parcel post."

We paid Mike a couple hundred dollars as a retainer on this case and made plans for a further meeting.

"He's just what we need for Jake," I told Rick on the way back to Charlotte. "The bastard has guts, knows what to do at the right time and I believe, if he's loyal, he'll play the a game just like we want him too."

"I told you, son, I only fix you up with the best," Rick said. I didn't say anything, but I remembered some of the trashy women he had tried to fix me up with in the past and I smiled.

For two weeks we kept in contact with Mike and developed a grand case on the rig owners in the current investigation. All the while my primary goal was to size up Mike for them and one big leaguer—Jake Foster. I had to get him to liking me in order to have unquestioned loyalty to put into the Jake operation. I closely watched his actions, listened intently to his every comment and finally decided he was a prime candidate for the job.

Rick and I hit him to help us with Jake. He had heard of Jake but could say little about him at the time. He accurately speculated that perhaps Burris was Jake's broker for this area since Burris always had the same unlimited quality of booze.

And the beauty of this situation was that Mike and Burris were good friends and regularly traded and cooperated in the whiskey business.

We were convinced that the booze being distributed by Burris was coming from Jake's organization. Its quality and availability were too stable to be ordinary. We also were convinced that Mike was now loyal to us as much as could be expected from anyone who would betray his fellow violators and turn to the law. He was feared by most violators so we didn't worry too much for his safety. I didn't expect Jake to ever really deal directly with Mike though, as there was no need for it. This was why he had developed his famous broker distribution.

Rick and I agreed on a basic strategy. We thought the trucks used on large deliveries through Jake's brokers came from the distillery after a deal was made by Burris. At least, we gambled on it. Burris talked to Mike enough to indicate such.

First, we would have to be willing to have Mike make numerous truckload purchases from Burris, or enough to enable us to trail, piecemeal, the truck back to its origin. This likely would take months. Such backtracking could only be done a little at a time. This plan involved the possibility of the purchase of thousands of gallons of booze. The government was too damned stingy to pay the tab, so Rick and I had to conspire with Mike for him to sell the stuff to his customers. By doing this, we were using a small fish to catch a big one, even though it meant participating in the bootlegging business.

This would have been a nightmare for the ATF hierarchy and a field day for the head hunters if they had known what we were doing. This didn't bother us in the slightest because we had no intention of telling either the first thing about what we were doing. It would be a simple matter of fabricating our daily reports to suit our plan. A system commonly known in ATF as "squirreling."

It was no trouble for Mike to get the loads from Burris. When he increased the size of his orders, sure enough, Burris stopped delivering the booze in his car. A strange fleet of trucks began appearing. A backtracking organization went into action, using several agents at the first nearby intersection to view the return routes of the trucks. The same driver was always involved, and according to Mike, when the driver says six words more, it will be half a dozen he has spoken. Such was the clannish, secretive and fierce dedication of Jake's outfit at every level.

Progress was extremely slow from the beginning, and slowed even more. The bastard driving the various trucks took every conceivable variety of return routes imaginable. Complicating the deal, too, was our knowledge that Jake had a network of his own two-way radios and even worse, we knew that he had a monitoring device for the various ATF bands.

It was later ascertained that he actually had a station with a voice-actuated receiver, complete with a recording device. He had only to check the unmanned station at his pleasure and play back everything that had been said on an ATF radio since his last check. True to the nature of Jake, however, even though there was a multitude of radio traffic involving other small and large violators all over the state, he never, never tipped them off. He would simply do his own mending and let them get their asses caught.

Rick, Mike, and I began having problems. The now steady stream of truckloads of booze, each numbering in the hundreds of gallons, began piling up on us. Mike was not a big enough operator to dispose of all this stuff to his regular customers. Too, I was using my personal funds to stockpile the whiskey, and had him to order more. At times, a load of five hundred gallons availed us nothing. If we were able to get the trucks even half a mile further on the backtrack we felt lucky and successful. To less determined men, this would have been fatal, because we knew the distillery could be anywhere, from ten miles away to hundreds.

Then I made a discovery that gave more encouragement than anything else had. The whiskey was usually still warm when delivered, meaning that the distillery was close enough so that the stuff wouldn't completely cool off enroute.

At one of our board meetings, Rick, Mike and I decided that something had to be done to dispose of the stuff to replenish our funds in order to carry on the operation. Mike had to enlarge his business. He had had sufficient customers but had to cut off some of them in two counties due to honest law enforcement pressure in one and his stubborn refusal to pay a crooked sheriff to allow him to operate in the other.

I made the decision that Mike should go back to his old customers and reestablish with them. My moral thoughts on the thing didn't bother me, because I considered it only an efficient part of an investigation to get the top, and besides, the old customers were still buying the stuff from someone else, anyway.

Mike was afraid of being caught in those two counties. Rick and I decided that we would make limited deliveries through the counties at certain sections where Mike might be caught. If Rick and I were ever stopped, we had only to show our badges and say that we had just seized the booze. A good setup, but still hazardous in many ways.

Months went by with slow progress. We had now backtracked the trucks about seven miles. Even this far out, the driver still had just that many more options on different routes to take.

One particular night, I had to make a run for Mike with him following from a safe distance in the government car so he could get his load of moonshine in the neighborhood of its destination and he could complete the delivery. Rick was absent that night.

The trip was to be about fifteen miles before it would be safe to swap back with Mike, who would take over just before reaching the destination. One thing bothered me. This was the county

189

with the crooked sheriff, who was especially bitter about Mike's telling him to kiss his ass concerning payola. He and his deputies knew most of the old hotrods that Mike used. I was determined not to let them stop me with this booze.

The truck came in about 9:00 p.m. and at 9:30 I left with Mike trailing me about two miles. I passed through an intersection well inside the risky county at normal speed. The old trap I drove didn't look like much but, like everything Mike had, it ran like hell.

From nowhere came the lights of a sheriff's car!

I downshifted on the old car and gave it hell. The chase was on. Mile after mile, it lasted and it looked like I would never outrun that prowl car, mainly because I was loaded and unfamiliar with these back roads. Finally, the two deputies in the car began shooting. Thankfully, no bullet hit a tire and, even better, none hit me in the back of the head. I silently cursed them. Now I knew what it felt like to be on the other side.

After many miles and more shooting, the deputies must have run out of ammunition. They began trying to catch me on curves and knock me off the road. Now they were playing my game and I was confident I could win this sort of fight.

But this was somewhat different because I didn't consider this operation worth a killing even if I didn't trust them. It would be hard to explain. It would blow the lid off this entire investigation. I could only hope to be lucky enough to catch them in a maneuver in which I could just put them out of action with no mortal damage.

But harder and harder they dueled, no doubt thinking they were about to catch Mike. My old hotrod now was really battered. It took considerable skill to keep it going with the beating these guys were giving me.

Finally, when they got alongside, I suddenly hit the brakes and dropped behind them. At something like one hundred mph plus, I wheeled hard left into the right rear of the prowl car. It made two or three one hundred-eighty degree spins in the road and slammed over an embankment backward.

I immediately slowed down and looked back. I saw the two men crawl out of the wreck's two front windows from its prone position on its top. Then the car burst into flames.

Very good, I thought. Neither of them could have been injured very much, as long as they scrambled up the bank and looked in my direction. I lurched the rear end of my car good-bye to them by spinning down the road as fast as I could.

Now I had to find my way back to my usual rendezvous with Mike near his home. There was no way I could meet him now otherwise. I finally made it and sat in the woods waiting for him. The thoughts crossed my mind that I could have gotten into real trouble over this little chase. Wouldn't the head hunters have a field day if they learned about it? But I wasn't worried after I saw neither of the officers was hurt. If ever confronted with it, I would, as always, "DENY THE ALLEGATIONS AND DAMN THE ALLE-GATORS."

Mike arrived and I explained what happened. "Get rid of this heap, Mike, you can never use it again."

He was very pleased in spite of the loss of his vehicle. He pounded me on the shoulder. "Damn," he said admiringly. "Any man who can outdrive the law as neatly as that ought to be road running full time. I'll get you a different car every day of the week as long as you teach those bribe-taking bastards of the law a lesson like you just did."

The truckloads kept coming. No other bad situations developed in my assistance to Mike in his deliveries. Progress bogged down in the backtracking.

Rick and I assessed our position. We felt now that we would eventually find the distillery, but we knew within reason that there would be no way that Jake or Knox could be incriminated. I had been nursing an idea that Jake could only be brought to the forefront by using his strength as a weakness against him. He was so cautious, so secret, so safe. I began thinking and believing that there must be some way this craving for super security could be used against him. Then it dawned on me. Distant drum beats of success started sounding deep in my cranium corridors.

We must drop the hint to him through Burris that an unnamed federal agent could be bribed by the right deal. Jake was accustomed to bribing local officials, but never had he more than dreamed of the spectacular accomplishment of bribing a federal agent. Herein might be a glimmer of hope for a case against this master criminal genius.

There had been no suspicion at all about the fiery crash of the county deputies' car. According to reports, only one of the men had a slight injury. But the prowl car had been demolished. So obviously, Rick and I were having a lot of fun on the side, too.

I was greatly enjoying this assignment that was keeping me one hundred and fifty miles away from my Raleigh office.

The seed about a federal agent possibly being on the take had been planted. Mike dropped it to Burris, who was certain to hit Jake with it. Sure enough, within forty-eight hours Burris came to Mike's home in a flurry. He handed over five one hundred dollar bills as a no-strings-attached token for Mike just to explore the idea. Mike had put it to Burris that such a deal would have to be worked through him.

This news came as a major breakthrough, mostly because Jake had at least made a contact, though indirectly. He had now authorized Burris to refer to him merely as "the man." Exhibiting his loyalty to us, Mike offered to surrender the five hundred dollars as evidence. I told him to keep it and to hell with it as evidence, since there was no way we could consider it as such. I made notes of the serial numbers, though I couldn't see how this could ever be used. What thrilled me was that we had found a weakness in the great moonshiner Jake.

On and on the truckloads kept coming. For a long while no further encouragement came from Jake concerning the bribery possibility. That didn't worry me. Jake worked so cautiously that he might ponder his next move in such a golden opportunity for six months, maybe longer.

Then a personal disaster hit me like a ton of bricks.

Grandy Boldt, my partner in Raleigh, died instantly at age forty-one of a heart attack. I was withdrawn from the case and sent back to Raleigh to handle the already heavy caseload of moonshiners, almost as big in volume as Jake, but certainly none as big in intellect and sophistication.

After the funeral, I went back to Charlotte and talked with Rick. We had such a thing going that it was sickening to have to give it up. We decided to select another member of the ATF racketeering squad, try to get him assigned to take my place and tell him the whole story. It proved difficult to do. Not many agents would dare carry on this type of operation for fear of the head hunters.

We finally selected Harold Cook, a seasoned and gutsy agent. I made arrangements with the man who was now my boss in Atlanta to assign him.

We met with Harold and detailed for him the total picture, with the exception of the delivery assistance that we had given Mike. We didn't tell him this because we were not sure that he would keep his mouth shut permanently.

Harold and Rick continued to push our investigation.

192

Harold was plenty good at this sort of thing and performed splendidly. Progress continued slowly in the backtracking strategy. I predicted the distillery was located within twenty miles of the home of Mike and that it would be found before too many more months.

I kept up with the investigation by telephone, mostly to Rick.

Finally, after about a year of leapfrog trailing, back- tracking and patience, a truck was followed to its return destination on a secluded farm in the boondocks. It circled a farmhouse then drove through automatically rising and lowering doors of the barn. In a few minutes, the driver left the barn and walked to the farmhouse and vanished inside. There was no further sign of activity.

For two weeks several agents maintained a surveillance of the premises from a vantage point about three hundred yards from the barn. During this period, an aircraft was kept aloft in radio contact to follow any vehicle emerging from the barn to its initial destination. The plane was successful in trailing a truck some sixty miles to a large warehouse where it picked up raw materials.

After about two weeks, scouts who systematically checked the area for foreign sign, specifically footprints, ranged beyond their normal boundary and discovered a team of agents lying in wait. Both fled and shouted warnings. A young agent gave chase and caught one. The other temporarily escaped. Instant radio communication brought bloodhounds to the scene. Between the bloodhounds and the airplane overhead, the second man was run down on foot and apprehended about two miles from the scene. Follow-up investigation eventually brought the arrest of two other men. Also arrested was the man posing as a tenant in the farmhouse whose only job was to act as guard.

None of these people were big in the operation. There was no evidence against Jake or his executive officer, Knox.

Under the barn, the agents found the entrance to the massive underground distillery. Nobody had ever seen anything quite so unbelievable before.

A Charlotte, North Carolina, newspaper screamed bold headlines about an elaborate giant underground distillery seized. Photographs showed the gigantic installation and it really proved incredible.

It was found about seventeen miles from the residence of

Mike, which accounted for the warmth of the booze that he received.

For days the area newspaper reported the hullabaloo surrounding the seizure and destruction or removal of the still. Sightseers by the thousands drove by the location. It was now my hope that the seizure would cause Jake to pursue his dream of bribing a federal agent. It worked, but several weeks passed before he made his move.

Knowing that Harold was the quarterback of the investigation, he finally made a direct telephone call to Harold, telling him he wanted to see him. I advised Harold to stake out agents to support his every move, and to wear hidden recording equipment on his person.

Jake met Harold in a motel near Charlotte and talked to him over thirty minutes. But he didn't mention the bribe, preferring to size up Harold, who did a beautiful job. From time to time they met and fenced with each other.

Finally, Jake hit him with it. He offered Harold a large retainer sum, so much per month, plus a year-end bonus if all continued well. This was all taped and agents hovered nearby covering every move.

Harold took several large payments from Jake, all of which were retained as evidence, along with complete tape recordings of all the conversations transpiring at the numerous meetings. Jake was taken to trial in the United States Court in Charlotte and forthwith convicted.

Even while Jake was in prison the operation continued.

The large distillery ultimately seized as a result of the work of Mike, Rick, Harold and me had operated for about nine years. Jake and his cohorts had made many millions with it.

There is no doubt in my mind that they had yet another underground distillery operating somewhere, which I believe is still operating to this day.

EPILOGUE

Many successful law enforcement officers learn that they must fight fire with fire at times. They are placed in a position of doing a difficult, and sometimes impossible, job while being hamstrung with antiquated constitutional amendments, emasculating court orders, bureaucratic bungling and beautifully designed and professionally stacked legal loopholes.

A good officer must have talents in the field of law enforcement approaching that of a lawyer, a psychologist, minister, be a physical marvel and be a con artist. He takes the chances of having his guts shot out and of losing his family because of prolonged absences from home.

Virtually all good officers have violated the laws in a technical sense, with no corrupt motives, in order to better enforce the statutes and by-pass unnecessary government regulations and procedures.

We could sit on our asses and do little. But crime would proliferate much more than it does now and more people would be murdered, raped, robbed and paralyzed in fear. Or we can take the long chances and do the best job. If we get by with it, we are heroes, which to the honorable officer means little. But it does mean a lot to know that you have accomplished your mission and made the country a safer place to live. It is self-satisfying and its own reward.

If we get caught with our hands in the cookie jar, we suffer. Supervisors who have been through it understand. But the news media, the head hunters and the prosecutors do not understand or else they think only of their own bag.

I'm not saying that the investigator, whether he be ATF, Secret Service, FBI, SBI, or otherwise, constantly violates a law in order to better enforce the laws. This is the exception rather than the rule. But it is done frequently.

An ATF agent who makes efforts comparable to the main characters in this book, should be entitled to retirement after ten years with full pay, like federal judges enjoy.

The most demoralizing factor, leaving most devastation in its wake, is the shameful failure of some judges, including federal

195

judges, who brazenly acquit or slap a big shot moonshiner on the wrist at times laughing and joking with him in open court, giving him, in effect, no sentence. Then thirty minutes later, they send some poor bastard who has no money to prison for five to ten years for the exact same crime. Even worse is for the agent to work his heart out for months to build a good case against a big criminal and then see him never even go to court.

Unbelievably, I have even seen a federal judge sentence such a criminal to stand up in court and shake hands with the officer who made the case against him, and promise to never violate the law again.

In another case, a criminal had shot at an officer and missed, although his intention was to kill. He was charged with assault, convicted and placed on a suspended sentence. The judge told him in open court: "Son, I'm going to place you on probation, but I'm here to tell you, if you had killed that officer, I would have been forced to send you to prison."

Big damn deal. **BIG DAMN DEAL.**

And this judge will be entitled to full retirement at $40,000 to $50,000 a year for life after ten years of such "service."

I am thankful that I performed my duties without having to take the life of anyone, although I have walked into the barrels of shotguns, pistols and have taken knives from the hands of dangerous suspectes. I have never owned a blackjack and never hit but two people with anything except my fists. Fists I have used and used effectively, but never without justification.

I have been injured eleven times, suffered two brain concussions, dozens of broken bones, been shot at on many occasions and I was also battered seriously in several automobile chases By the grace of God, I survived it all.

For many years I worked in districts where the courts destroyed all my efforts and the money that the U.S. Government spent went for naught. This contributed to the fatal demoralization of a strong spirit. The last year, my efforts were not worth a damn. My health had deteriorated to the point where I could no longer keep up. Thus, I retired.

If I had the opportunity to advise new agents and officers, I would tell them: Do your very best job with no selfish motives, and if you get backed into a corner because of some unorthodox methods, always remember to **"DENY THE ALLEGATIONS AND DAMN THE ALLEGATORS."**

DEPARTMENT OF THE TREASURY
BUREAU OF ALCOHOL, TOBACCO AND FIREARMS
WASHINGTON. D.C. 20226

OFFICE OF
THE DIRECTOR

REFER TO

March 30, 1973

Dear Joe,

It is hard to realize eighteen years have passed since you came to Wilkesboro full of desire to "get with it" and that is just what you did. I am sure as I look back that your enthusiasm was a good example for all of us. Maybe we can get together some day soon and spend a day or two just covering the highlights.

Joe, I am sorry I can't be present in Dunn tonight. It would have pleased both Zola and me if we could have come. But the Lord willing we do hope to see you soon.

I want to thank you for the committment you made to ATF and more specifically the loyalty and cooperation you gave me in Wilkesboro.

I want to wish you the best in your new career and may God bless and keep you.

Sincerely,

John West

DEPARTMENT OF THE TREASURY
BUREAU OF ALCOHOL, TOBACCO AND FIREARMS

Office of Inspection
Post Office Box 6199
Washington, D.C., 20044

OFFICE OF
INSPECTION

(202)-964-8731

March 30, 1973

Refer to

Dear Joe:

    I regret not being able to attend your party tonight.
Nothing would please me more than to join your many friends
in wishing you a long, happy and healthy party.

    When I first came to North Carolina in 1963 you were
one of the few people in the State that I knew. As we
became better acquainted over the years I developed a
sincere respect for your dedication to ATF and your loyalty
and support in all that we tried to do. You can take a
lot of pride in the many real accomplishments during your
career. Special Agents with your dedication and ability
are an asset to any organization. I appreciate the opportunity to have shared part of your career in North Carolina.

    Mary joins me in wishing you happiness, health, and
continued success in all endeavors of life.

Sincerely,

Jarvis

Jarvis Brewer

OFFICE OF
THE DIRECTOR

DEPARTMENT OF THE TREASURY
BUREAU OF ALCOHOL, TOBACCO AND FIREARMS
WASHINGTON, D.C. 20226

March 30, 1973

REFER TO

Dear Joe:

On this occasion of your retirement, let me take this opportunity to thank you for your contribution to ATF. From your record and from those who know you I am aware you are committed totally to the cause of good law enforcement and you have vigorously pursued this committment in ATF.

Starting out in Wilkesboro, North Carolina in 1955, you have since been in four other posts of duty. This points out your willingness to go where you were needed. Your record of making cases against major violators is commendable.

I want to wish you the best for your future and again thanks for a job well done.

Sincerely yours,

Rex D. Davis

Rex D. Davis